CAN YOU COMPLETE THE PUZZLE?

(A Journey Towards Spiritual Growth and Direction)
Volume Three

Verdree B. Stanley

WestBow
PRESS
A DIVISION OF THOMAS NELSON

WestBow Press books may be ordered through booksellers or by contacting:

WestBow Press
A Division of Thomas Nelson
1663 Liberty Drive
Bloomington, IN 47403
www.westbowpress.com
1-(866) 928-1240

ISBN: 978-1-4497-8554-3 (sc)
ISBN: 978-1-4497-8555-0 (e)

Library of Congress Control Number: 2013902910

Printed in the United States of America

WestBow Press rev. date: 2/20/2013

Table of Contents

Preface

The Lord himself warned, "In the world you shall have tribulations" (John 16: 33). When attempts are made in understanding the Bible, it can become a puzzling experience. Learning what the Bible is all about in its truest form is a journey. Too often, the approach used to interpret the Bible consists in taking every phrase and every sentence as if that small portion of the text contained theological dogma in and of itself, and taking each saying as if it were to be understood in a literal manner. In such an approach, phrases and short sentences from the Scriptures are cited to support bias theories and ideas when these phrases and sentences do not carry the meaning imposed upon them. It is the task, therefore, of each person to make every effort to understand properly and critically the teachings of the various biblical materials. God wants us to choose to love him freely, even when that choice involves pain, because we are committed to him, not to our own good feelings and rewards. He wants us to cleave to him, even when we have every reason to deny him.

Sample Puzzle

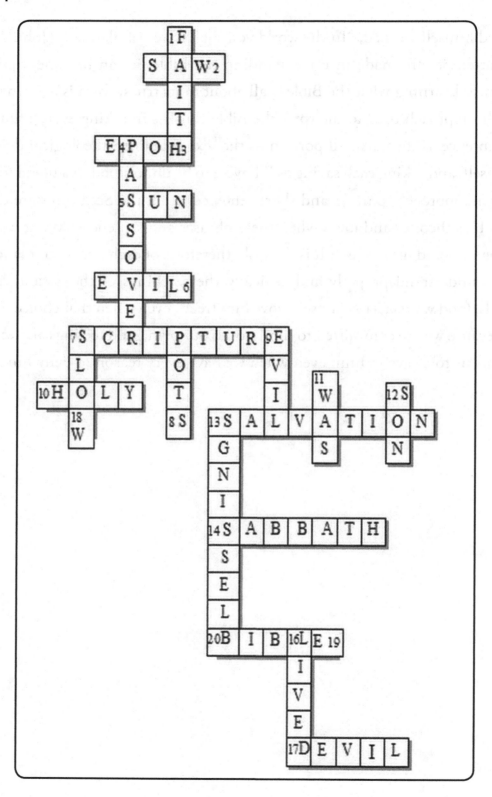

Answers to Sample Crossword Puzzle

ACROSS: (FORWARD)

5. Sun

7. Scripture

10. Holy

13. Salvation

14. Sabbath

17. Devil

ACROSS: (BACKWARDS)

2. Was

3. Hope

6. Live

19. Bible

DOWN :(DOWNWARD)

1. Faith

4. Passover

9. Evil

12. Son

16. Lived

UP: (UPWARD)

8. Stop

11. Saw

20. Blessings

UP: (BACKWARD)

18. Slow

Note:

Each crossword can be 1) Across forwards, 2) Across backwards, 3) Downwards or 4) Upwards. Your starting point will begin with the number located in the box. Please keep in mind that all completed words are not always from left to right. Also, it is important that you read the question and search the scriptures for the correct answer.

Tools Needed For Completing This Book:

- Holy Bible (King James Version).
- Pencil, Eraser, Note Pad.
- Biblical Concordance.
- Webster Dictionary
- All scriptures are from the Holy Bible.
- The answer to each puzzle is in each given scripture.
- Definitions of terms are taken from; Biblical Commentaries, Biblical Dictionaries and Webster's Dictionaries.

Note:

Working through each puzzle will bring blessings your way.

New Features in Volume Three

1. Each crossword puzzle is larger for better focus and concentration.

2. The answers to each puzzle are located on the back pages of the book.

3. Each crossword puzzle question can be used as a preaching reference tool, teaching reference too, group study reference tool or personal meditation tool for growth.

4. I believe that working through each puzzle will enhance a person's well-being in life.

Genesis

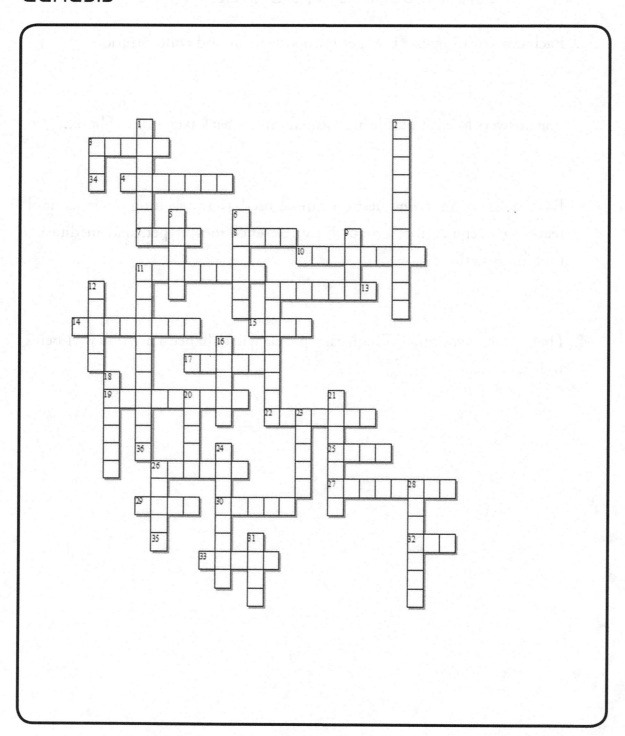

Genesis - Questions

Across: (Forward)

3 - An_____spoke to Jacob during the dream. ch: 31

4 - Abraham had become a very_____man. ch: 21

7 - Lift up your_____. ch: 40

8 - It is clear that Jacob spent very little time with_____. ch: 30

10 - And you, be ye_____. ch: 9

11 - Egyptians used to_____dead bodies. ch: 50

14 - Joseph wanted_____to receive a greater blessing. ch: 48

15 - Everything that God does is_____. ch: 4

17 - The journey to_____took three days. ch: 22

19 - _____was very kind to Abraham. ch: 20

22 - _____; means shelter. ch: 33

25 - Israel is Jacob's_____as the head of the family. ch: 47

26 - Joseph's first question was about his_____. ch: 43

27 - Barak came from the tribe of_____. ch: 49

29 - Abram went to Egypt because he needed_____. ch: 12

30 - _____wanted to impress Rachel. ch: 29

32 - The writer mentions Sarah's_____when she died. ch: 23

33 - Leah was Jacob's _____wife. ch: 46

Across: (Backwards)

13 - _____. Black stuff people would get from the ground to use like cement ch: 11

Down:

1 - The servant was still praying when_____came out. ch: 24

2 - We do not know whether_____usually wore veils. ch: 38

5 - And he sent forth a_____. ch: 8

6 - God told Abram that his descendants would be_____in Egypt for 400 years. ch: 15

9 - Abram listened to his_____. ch: 16

12 - Joseph wanted to send the_____to Canaan quickly. ch: 42

16 - But Noah found_____. ch: 6

18 - Esau's first two wives did not come from Abraham's_____. ch: 36

20 - _____. It is also like a description or picture for us. ch: 3

21 - And the first day consisted of evening and_____. ch: 5

23 - Abram's descendants would be so many that nobody would be able to_____them. ch:13

24 - _____; means "son of my right hand" ch: 35

28 - This passage shows how important_____was in God's plan. ch: 18

31 - Jacob thought that_____would perhaps still be angry after the first gift. ch: 32

Up: (Backwards)

11 - Abram did not agree to keep the_____. ch: 14

34 - And they went in unto Noah into the_____. ch: 7

35- And unto them were sons born after the_____. ch: 10

Exodus

Exodus – Questions

Across: (Forward)

8 - The Lord came down to the_____of Mount Sinai. ch: 19

11 - Then Moses listened to_____. ch: 18

21 - Rules for the_____party. ch: 12

23 - Moses and Aaron bring_____out of the water. ch: 8

24 - The "Tent of_____" ch: 40

28 - Oholiab is the son of_____. ch: 35

31 - _____; Aaron's son. ch: 6

Across: (Backwards)

5 - If a man finds a_____, he must cover it. ch: 21

9 - Seven days went by after the Lord had made the water in the_____into blood. ch: 7

10 - The place where you_____is Holy ground. ch: 3

12 - Cover the boards with_____and make gold rings. ch: 26

15 - Moses'_____shines. ch: 34

16 - Do your work for_____days. ch: 23

32 - Keep the Sabbath_____because it is a Holy day for you. ch: 31

Down:

1 - So I will make the_____of meeting, Holy and separate.. ch: 29

2 - The Israelites worked with bricks and_____. ch: 1

3 - These rings would hold the_____to carry the table. ch: 37

4 - Make the_____out of gold and out of blue, purple, red and white. ch: 28

13 - The Israelites ate the_____for 40 years. ch: 16

14 - Put one flower not yet open, under the_____pair of branches. ch: 25

26 - The water was like a_____on their right and on their left side. ch: 14

29 - Pieces of_____fall on the whole country of Egypt. ch: 9

Up: (Backwards)

6 - The_____of every firstborn son in Egypt. ch: 11

7 - Moses took the_____of Joseph with him. ch: 13

17 - Exodus continues the story of Jacob's family in_____.)See reference page).

18 - For the tabernacle, the workers made boards that_____up. ch: 36

19 - Moses wants to see God's_____. ch: 33

20 - You must make the same_____of bricks as you made before. ch: 5

22 - The south side of the_____was 46 meters long. ch: 38

25 - Exodus is a_____book. (See reference page).

27 - This oil is to burn in the_____. ch: 27

30 - It must have_____in it and it must be clean and Holy. ch: 30

33- You must kill_____who has sex with an animal. ch: 22

34 - Exodus is the_____book of the Bible. (See reference page).

Leviticus

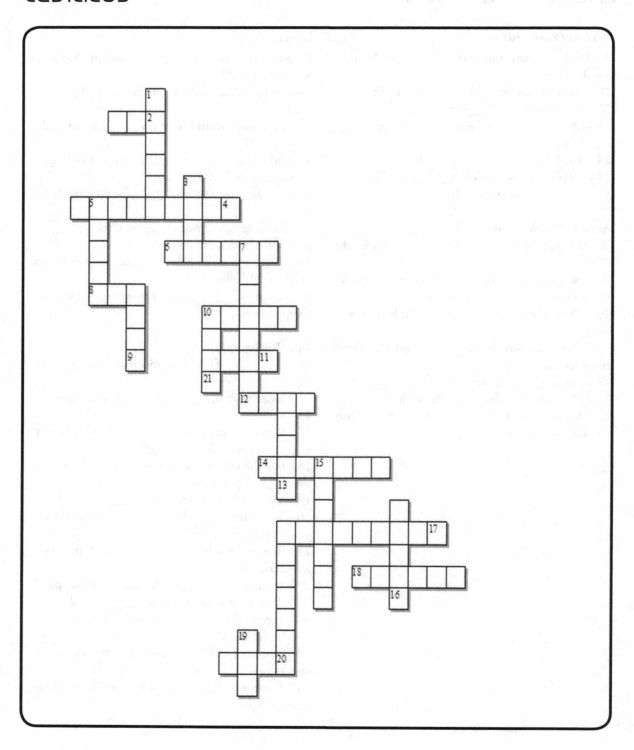

Leviticus - Questions

Across: (Forward)

6 - _____; is a plant. ch: 14

8 - Moses offered "the bull" as a"_____offering" ch: 8

10 - Moses and Aaron;_____the people. ch: 9

12 - _____. The Hebrew word for relative. ch: 25

14 - The people must_____the priests and their families. ch: 21

18 - _____was a false god. ch: 20

Across: (Backwards)

2 - God did not want the Israelites to_____ blood. ch: 17

4 - On the "Day of_____" the Israelites did not work; they do not eat food. ch: 16

11 - The Hebrew words for "On the alter" really means "On the_____" ch: 7

17 - _____. A bad thing that someone says against God. ch: 24

20 - People_____corn in order to clean it. ch: 26

Down:

1 - To_____something to the Lord is a very serious matter. ch: 27

3 - Be Holy, because I am_____. ch: 19

5 - The Priests tells the person to live alone for seven days then for another_____days. ch: 13

7 - "Whole_____" Name of Sacrifice. ch: 1

15 - The book of Leviticus also describes the duties of_____during the time of the Old Testament. (see reference page).

19 - The book of Leviticus is about the_____of God. (see reference page).

22 - "Sin_____" Many ancient religions used it. God did not allow his people to do it. ch: 18

Up: (Backwards)

9 - "_____Offering" The Priests burn a small part of it on the alter as a reminder. ch: 6

13 - "_____offering" A person gives, to say, "Thank-you" ch: 22

16 - Food that is_____and food that is unclean. ch: 11

21 - The woman is unclean because she_____ during the birth. ch: 12

Numbers

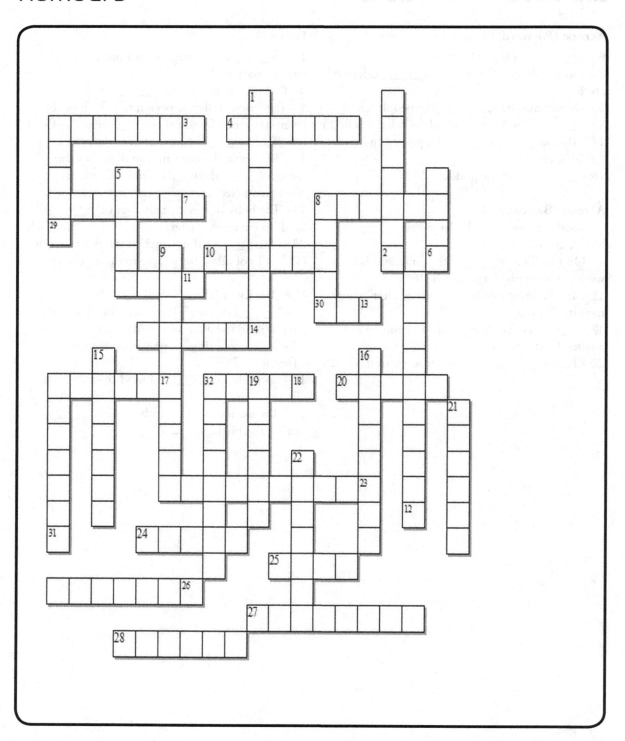

Numbers – Questions

Across: (Forward)

4 - Moses talks to God on_____of the Israelites. ch: 14

8 - We can compare the Numbers in the first and_____censuses. ch: 26

10 - When the_____men returned, they gave a report about the promised land, to Moses and the Israelites. ch: 13

20 - "Holy_____" It was kept in God's tent. The priests mixed it with dust. Also, he mixed it with ink. ch: 5

24 - One of Levi's tribe job; was to_____God's tent, so that the other Israelites did not come too close. ch: 18

25 - Balak takes Balaam to_____mountain. ch: 23

Across: (Backwards)

3 - The people celebrated the "_____ Festival" 50 days after the Passover. ch: 28

7 - The people saw that Eleazar was_____the High Priest's clothes. ch: 20

11 - God allowed any person who had killed another person by accident to go to a "_____ town" ch: 35

13 - The Israelites did not obey God completely. They did not force_____the inhabitants of Canaan to leave. ch: 33

14 - The Hebrew name for the book of Numbers is "In the_____" (See reference page).

17 - In these verses the author recorded the names of the male Israelites and the_____Midianite. ch: 25

18 - This book contains_____, instructions, poems and prophecies. (See reference page).

23 - The_____complained about life in the desert. (See reference page).

26 - This is the longest_____in the Old Testament apart from Psalms 119. ch: 7

27 - This passage refer to events during the month before the census. It is about the second_____. ch: 9

28 - _____. Moses' sister. ch: 12

Down:

1 - _____had five daughters and no sons. ch: 27

5 - Each leader_____his name on his stick. ch: 17

9 - Levi's tribe had to bring_____; then the Israelites had to put their hands on Levi's tribe. ch: 8

15 - This last chapter describes God's new laws about_____women and the land that they inherited. ch: 36

16 - There were three groups of_____in Levi's tribe. ch: 4

19 - It was the custom to share the_____between the soldiers and the people who did not fight. ch: 31

21 - God wanted the Israelites to divide the land_____. ch: 34

22 - Every Israelite had to sew_____onto their clothes. ch: 15

32 - During the "Festival of_____" the priests sacrificed more bulls and male sheep than during all other occasions. ch: 29

Up: (Backwards)

2 - The first generation did not enter the_____ land. (See reference page).

6 - What people must do after they have touched a dead_____. ch: 19

12 - When God gave his Spirit to the 70 leaders, they all_____. ch: 11

29 - The book begins two years after the Israelites had escaped from the country called_____. (See reference page).

30 - The Israelites used the word_____to describe the place where people go after death. ch: 16

31 - It was very important to keep a_____to God. ch: 30

Deuteronomy

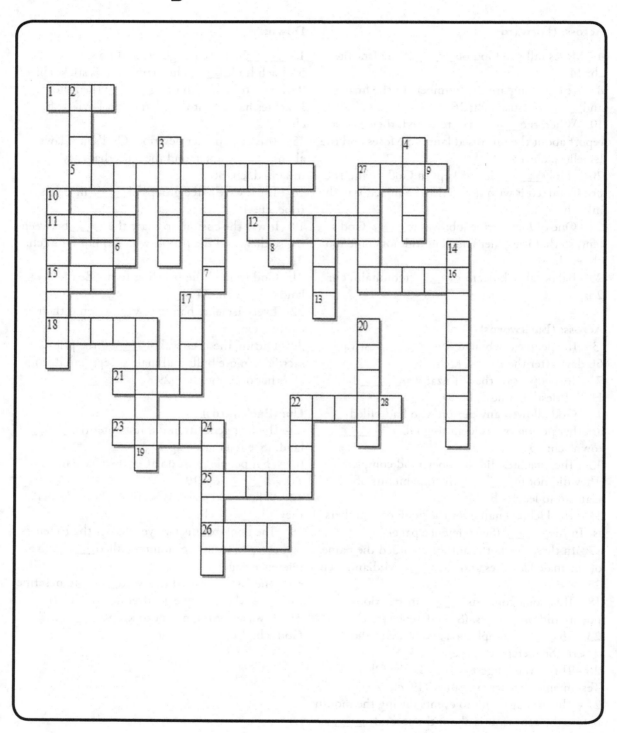

Deuteronomy - Questions

Across: (Forward)

1 - The young_____that the people made from gold. ch: 9

6 - Moses will die on Mount_____. ch: 32

11 - God offers_____or death. ch: 30

12 - On the other side of the_____river is the country called Canaan. (See reference page).

15 - A woman must not wear the clothes of a_____. A man must not wear the clothes of a woman. ch: 22

23 - The three special parties are; Passover,_____, and Tents. ch: 16

Across: (Backwards)

5 - _____. It is a book about remembering. (See reference page).

9 - At the end of every seven years, you must forget about every_____. ch: 15

16 - God's ten special_____. ch: 5

18 - Moses chose_____special cities to the east of the Jordan river. ch: 4

21 - If you obey the Lord your God, all_____ things will happen to you. ch: 28

25 - You must not become a servant of_____and obey him. ch: 18

26 - The_____words of Moses to the families of Israel. ch: 33

28 - Be careful to obey the_____of his promise. ch: 29

Up: (Backwards)

7 - You must burn their_____gods in a fire. ch: 7

8 - _____the Lord your God. ch: 6

13 - Moses tells the Israelites which_____to eat. ch: 14

19 - The_____of one man is not enough to check a bad thing. ch: 19

Down:

2 - _____the Lord's rules. ch: 26

3 - The writer of the book of Deuteronomy is_____. (See reference page).

10 - Then Moses_____Mount Nebo. ch: 34

14 - Watch for false gods and false_____. ch: 13

17 - The_____must be a man from Israel. ch: 17

22 - Rules about murder, marriage and_____, who refuse to obey. ch: 21

27 - Keep the_____prepared for God. ch: 23

Down: (Backwards)

4 - Always be ready to_____the Lord your God as his servants. ch: 10

20 - Do not tie up the_____of a cow while she walks on your corn to prepare it for you. ch: 25

24 - And when you have crossed the river; you must put those_____on Mount Ebal. ch: 27

Joshua

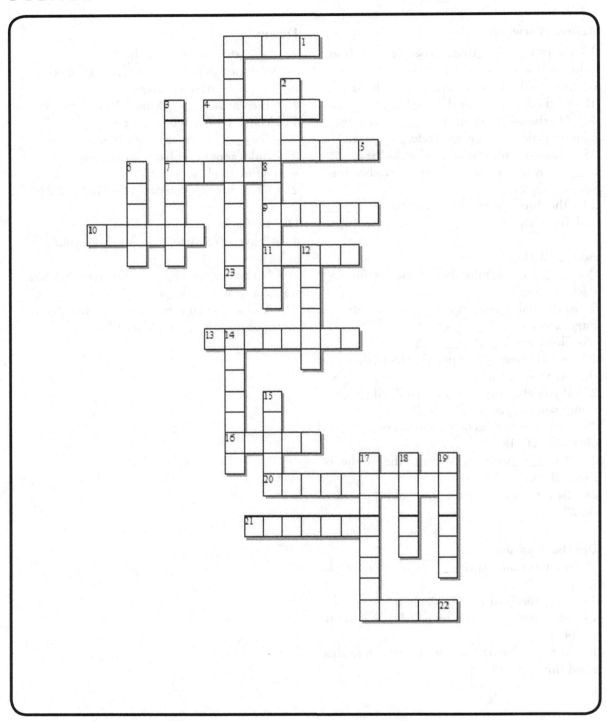

Joshua - Questions

Across: (Forward)

4 - The Israelites became friends with their enemies from_____. ch: 9

5 - The man was standing in front of Joshua and had a_____in his hand. ch: 5

7 - There were three "Cities of_____" on either side of the river Jordan. ch: 20

9 - _____; Was the place where the Anakites lived. ch: 14

10 - Joshua knew the power of_____. (See reference page).

11 - _____. The son of Carmi. ch: 7

13 - The two and a half tribes built an alter at_____. ch: 22

16 - Joshua_____God's law to the people. ch: 8

21 - The "Tribe of_____" was near lake Galilee. ch: 19

Across: (Backwards)

1 - Joshua was a helper to_____. (See reference page).

20 - Joshua led the army against the_____. (See reference page).

22 - The tribes of Reuben, Gad and Manasseh, are lands located east of the Jordan_____. ch: 13

Down:

2 - Joshua's name in the Hebrew language means; "The_____is my Saviour" (See reference page).

3 - The Israelites defeat the_____. ch: 10

6 - Only Joshua and_____brought good news back. (See reference page).

8 - The tribe of Joseph was divided between his two sons_____and Manasseh. ch: 16

12 - Manasseh was the first born son of_____. ch: 17

14 - Joshua was one of 12 men that Moses sent in secret to look at the_____land. (See reference page).

15 - Benjamin was a_____tribe. ch: 18

17 - Joshua_____the people about several things. ch: 23

18 - The priests had to show their_____. ch: 3

19 - Some kings in_____became afraid of the Israelites. ch: 11

Up:

23- In this story the number "7" shows us that God was giving the_____. ch: 6

Judges

Judges - Questions

Across: (Forward)

5 - In this section, the writer says there is no king. Everyone did what_____right to him. ch: 17

7 - Many Judges had strong_____. (See reference page).

9 - The Israelites did not want one tribe to_____ completely. ch: 21

11 - When the main army saw the smoke, it would_____around. ch: 20

15 - Abimelech, means my father is a_____. ch: 8

16 - The Judges were very_____. (See reference page).

17 - The men from Ephraim's tribe_____. ch: 12

Across: (Backwards)

4 - The writer then tells us what the book is about. The people left God; they did evil things and they praised the_____. ch: 2

6 - _____; means "The house of God" ch: 1

12 - _____; He killed 600 Philistines with a sharp stick. ch: 3

18 - Havvoth Jair, means Jair's_____that consisted of tents. ch: 10

19- The wet_____would be more useful than a dry one would be. ch: 15

Down:

1 - People did not choose Judges for their_____; God chose them. (See reference page).

3 - _____; The wife of Heber, the Kenite. ch: 5

8 - He cut up his_____limb by limb into 12 pieces. ch: 19

10 - Mount Hermon separated this area from_____. ch: 18

13 - The Israelites soon forgot about Deborah's_____and they behaved in their old ways again. ch: 6

14 - There were_____Judges (Leaders). (See reference page).

Up:

2 - But then a woman threw down a heavy_____; it hit him on the head and it broke his skull. ch: 9

Up: (Backwards)

20- The book of Judges is like a_____. (See reference page).

Ruth

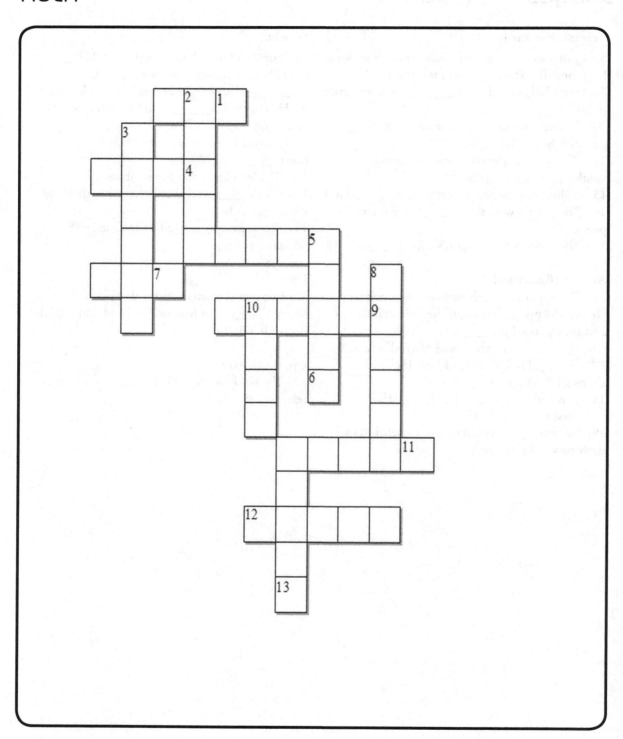

Ruth - Questions

Across: (Forward)

12 - This is the family tree of_____. ch: 4

Across: (Backwards)

1 - These_____measures of barley he gave to me; ch: 3

4 - _____; A short form of Obadiah meaning, servant of God. ch: 4

5 - Boaz asked his servant who is that young_____? ch: 2

7 - And she_____at the place of his feet until morning. ch: 3

9 - Boaz announces redemption and the_____ respond. ch: 4

11 - Ruth came to Boaz's field to collect_____. (See reference page).

Down:

2 - _____was Ruth's husband's mother. (See reference page).

3 - _____; A type of grain. ch: 3

8 - _____; To pay another person's debts and to protect them when they cannot help themselves. ch: 3

10 - The events in the book of_____happened over 3000 years ago. (See reference page).

Up:

6 - The book of Ruth is about a young_____. (See reference page).

13 - _____; To get what other people leave. ch: 3

1st Samuel

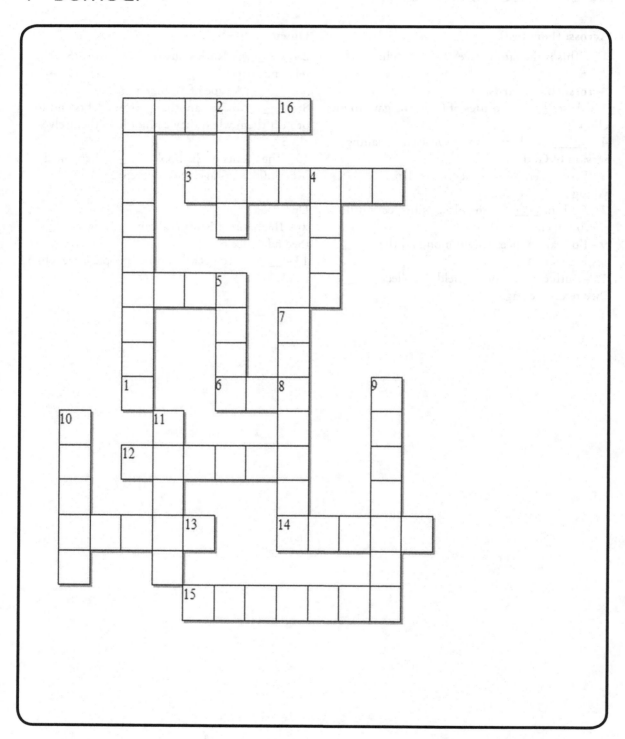

1st Samuel - Questions

Across: (Forward)

3 - God_____Saul as king. ch: 15

12 - The people ask_____to appoint a king. (See reference page).

14 - Hannah_____Samuel to God. ch: 1

15 - Saul becomes_____of David. ch: 18

16- Samuel was the last of the_____; he was also Prophet and a Priests. (See reference).

Across: (Backwards)

5 - The glory has_____Israel. ch: 4

8 - The Philistines returned the_____of God to Israel. ch: 6

13 - 1st Samuel tells the story of the_____king of Israel. (See reference page).

16- Samuel was the last of the_____; he was also Prophet and a Priests. (See reference).

Down:

1 - For_____Israel had no king. (See reference page). (Backwards)

2 - Samuel the prophet_____. ch: 25

4 - Saul and his_____die. ch: 31

6 - David refuses to_____Saul. ch: 24

7 - David and_____. ch: 17

9 - Saul looks for his father's_____. ch: 9

10 - Samuel did not_____the book; he died before the end of it. (See reference page).

11 - Samuel anoints_____. ch: 16

2nd Samuel

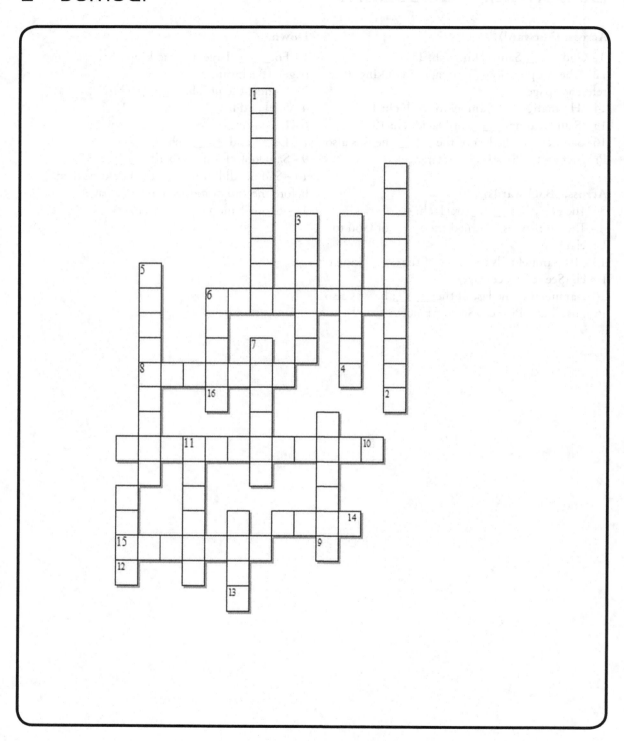

2nd Samuel - Questions

Across: : (Forward)

6 - _____; They lived in the land between southern Israel and the country of Egypt. ch: 1

8 - _____; metal, wood or hard leather. ch: 1

15 - _____; had a beautiful sister, her name was Tamar. ch: 13 (See reference page).

Across: (Backwards)

10 - _____; He had fallen and hurt his feet. ch: 9 (See reference page).

14 - The book of 2nd Samuel is about_____ David. (See reference page).

Up:

2 - The_____spoke and wrote in the Hebrew language. ch: 1

4 - David_____the Lord. ch: 22

9 - Zeruiah was David's_____. ch:2 (See reference page).

12 - David wins many_____. ch: 8 (See reference page).

13 - The book of 1st and 2nd Samuel use to be one_____. (See reference page).

Up: (Backwards)

16 - David builds an_____to the Lord. ch: 24 (See reference page).

Down:

1 - David had sex with a married woman named_____. (See reference page).

3 - David's men_____and kill Absalom. ch: 18

5 - David brings the "Ark of God" to_____. ch: 6

7 - Absalom wanted to become king, but_____ had anointed him as the king. ch: 15

11 - _____; A royal city, it was close to the river Jabbok. ch: 12 (See reference page).

1ˢᵗ Kings

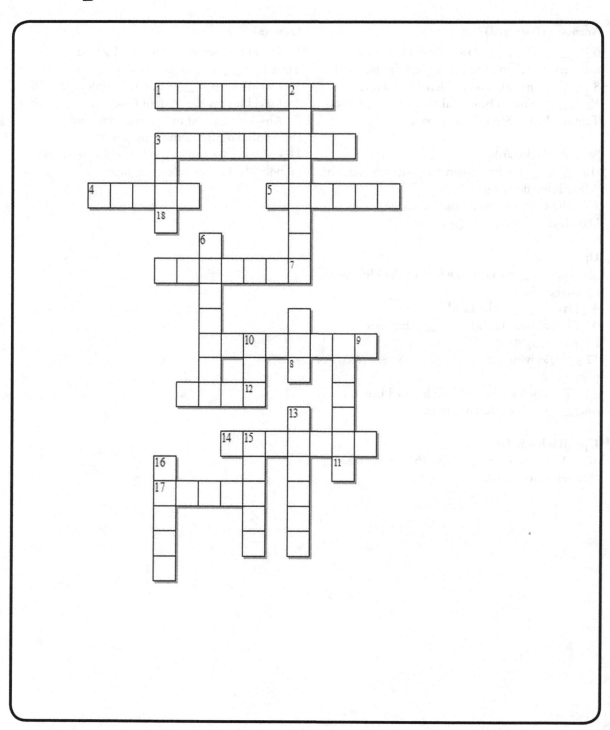

1st Kings – Questions

Across: (Forward)

1 - There is a book that reports about the kings of Israel; they wrote about everything else that king_____did. 14

3 - David told Solomon that some people were_____. ch: 1

4 - Michal, Abigail, Bathsheba, Haggith; were the_____ of David. ch: 1

5 - Solomon prays for_____. ch: 3

14 - "_____poles" Idols on a tall stick. (See reference page).

17 - The book of 1st Kings records how Solomon became king_____David. (See reference page).

Across: (Backwards)

7 - 1st Kings is about the_____of the people called Israelites. (See reference page).

9 - _____; was the first king of Judah. (See reference page).

12 - Before they built the temple, the ark was in a_____. ch: 8

Down:

2 - David had many children;_____was the oldest son. ch: 1

6 - 1st Kings begins with the story of_____, (See reference page).

10 - After Solomon died, the country called Israel became_____countries. (See reference page).

13 - The northern part of the country remained_____. (See reference page).

15 - "Become_____" in the Hebrew Bible; "have a change of mind" ch: 8

16 - The southern part of the country was_____. (See reference page).

Up:

8 - The ark was a_____. ch: 8 (See reference page).

11 - The_____had five parts. ch: 7

18- Ravens_____Elijah. ch: 17

2nd Kings

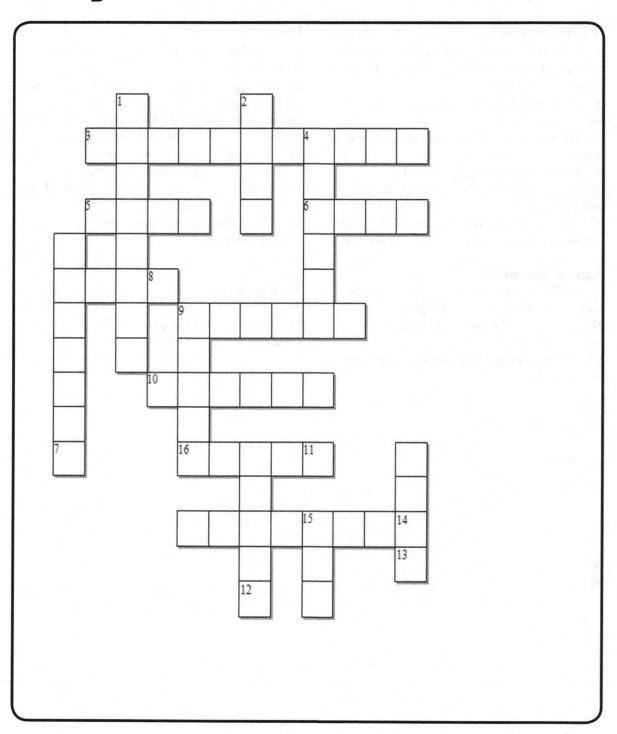

2nd Kings - Questions

Across: (Forward)

3 - _____; captain of the guard. ch: 25

5 - Elisha appointed_____king of Israel. (See reference page).

6 - The Israelites did not listen to God; they became slaves in their_____. ch: 17

9 - God did not allow Elijah to die, instead Elijah went up to_____. (See reference page).

10 - _____; was a captain of the foreign army. ch: 5

Across: (Backwards)

8 - Elisha saw Elijah rise to heaven in a vehicle of_____. (See reference page).

11 - 2nd Kings continues the story of the nations of Israel and_____. (See reference page).

14 - Queen_____tried to kill the father; royal family. (See reference page).

Up:

7 - 2nd Kings describes how the kings of these nations_____to obey God's law. (See reference page).

12 - Elisha caused a dead_____to live. ch: 4

13 - Elisha made poisonous food_____. ch: 4

16- _____, was seven years old when the army captains killed Queen Athaliah.)See reference page).

Down:

1 - _____; he had some kind of disease; boils; painful lumps under the skin. ch: 20

2 - Jehu kills the prophet of_____. ch: 10

4 - Elijah's companion was a man named_____. (See reference page).

15 - The_____that the man lost. ch: 6

1st Chronicles

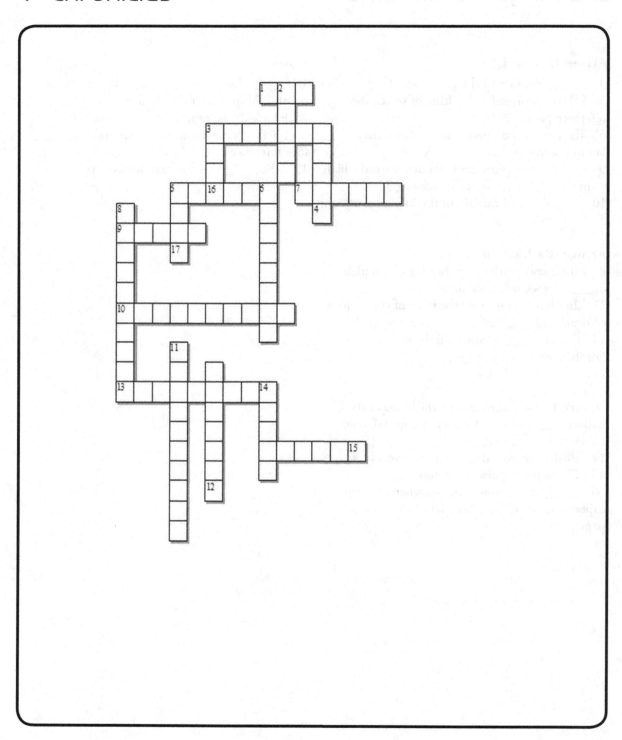

1st Chronicles - Questions

Across: (Forward)

1 - The family of_____. ch: 2

3 - Some christian_____say that Ezra received help from the prophets Haggai, Zechariah and Malachi. (See reference page).

5 - The prayer of David is a beautiful prayer, it is a prayer of_____. ch: 29

7 - The writer makes a list; who came from Noah's_____. (See reference page).

9 - _____; he became king of Tyre; his father Abibaal, was king of Tyre. ch: 14 (See reference page).

10 - The writer says that all_____are God's people. (See reference page).

13 - _____; was either a brother or a son of Ahihud. He went to the country called Moab. ch: 8 (See reference page).

Across: (Backwards)

15 - The writer of the book of Chronicles seems to be a_____; he writes about such things as Temple, Prayer, Worship of God. (See reference)

Down:

2 - _____; had four sons, Nadab, Abihu, Eleazar and Ithamar. ch: 24 (See reference page).

6 - _____; they lived in a town called Gedor; descendants of Edom. ch: 4 (See reference page).

8 - _____means, a list of events. (See reference page).

11 - _____; his other name was Jeconiah. ch: 3 (See reference page).

14 - Hezron's son Caleb is not the same as the Caleb who was with_____. ch: 2 (See reference page).

Up:

4 - The writer gives a list of_____. (See reference page).

12 - The books of Chronicle are_____books. (See reference page).

16- Jewish tradition , say that_____wrote Chronicles. (See reference page).

17 - The book of Chronicles usually appears as the_____book in the Hebrew Old Testament. (See reference page).

2nd Chronicles

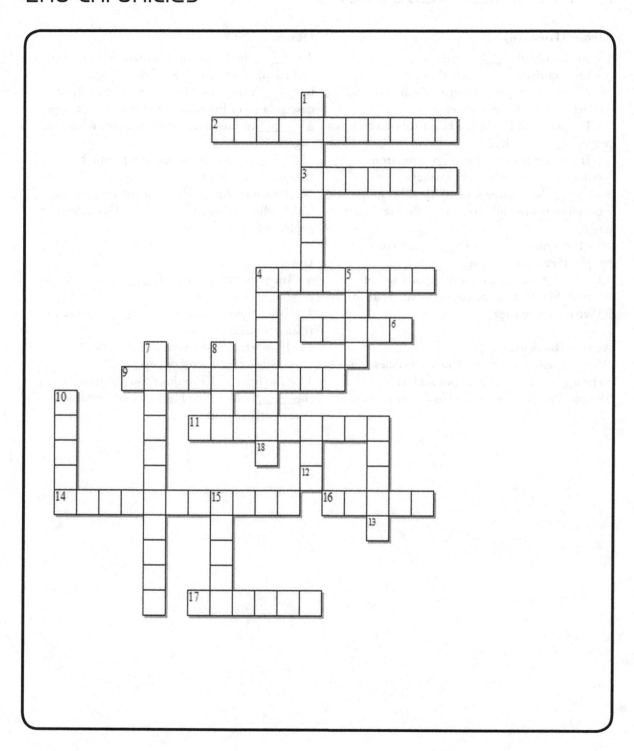

2ⁿᵈ Chronicles – Questions

Across: (Forward)

3 - 2nd Chronicles continues the history of Israel through the rule of king_____. (See reference page).

4 - _____; when he became strong, he turned from the Lord. ch: 12

9 - The ancient translation is called the_____. (See reference page).

11 - Israel_____from Judah. ch: 10

14 - _____; son of Sargon, attached Judah. ch: 32 (See reference page).

16 - The visit of the Queen of_____. ch: 9 (See reference page).

17 - Solomon built the_____. (See reference page).

Across: (Backwards)

2 - The two books of Chronicles were one book until there was a_____into the Greek language. (See reference page).

6 - Uzziah became_____of his power and this caused him to sin. ch: 26

Down:

1 - _____; it probably refers to a type of ship. It appears several times in the Bible. ch: 9 (See reference page).

5 - The_____of the Law. ch: 34 (See reference page).

7 - _____; was the 4th king of Judah. ch: 17

8 - Solomon began to build the temple in the 4th year of his_____. ch: 3

10 - The cloud of God's glory_____the temple. ch: 5

Down: (Backward)

15 - The writer of Chronicles lived after the_____. (See reference page).

Up:

12 - _____; was Jehoshaphat's father. ch: 20

13 - The Israelites had come back to their country after 70_____. (See reference page).

18 - Solomon married a_____of the king of Egypt. ch: 8

Ezra

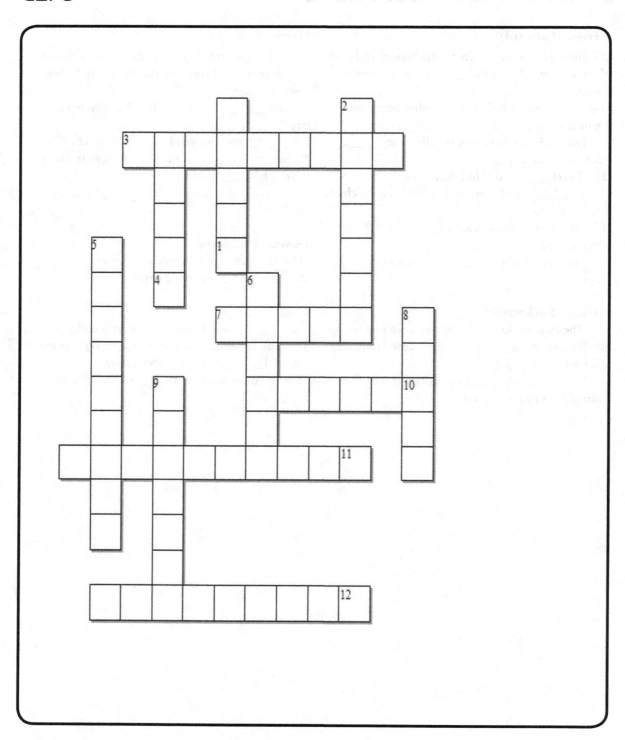

Ezra - Questions

Across: (Forward)

3 - The Jews started to build a temple (House of God) in_____. (See reference page).

7 - God sent Ezra to_____the people so that they would become God's special people again. (See reference page).

Across: (Backwards)

10 - _____; he gave honour to many false gods. ch: 6

11 - King_____gave a letter to Ezra. ch: 7

12 - Ezra recorded the list of people who returned from exile in_____. ch: 2

Up:

1 - King_____allowed God's people to return to Judah in order to build the temple. ch: 1

4 - There were_____special holidays to worship God during that month. ch: 3

Down:

2 - The_____month was very special to the Jews. ch: 3

6 - The book of Ezra in the Bible tells us that the king of_____allowed the Jews to return to their own land. (See reference page).

8 - Not all the Jews returned to_____. (See reference page).

9 - Ezra recorded the names of men who had_____wives. ch: 10

Down: (Backwards)

5 - _____; the son of Jehiel, said to Ezra; we have not obeyed God. ch: 10

Nehemiah

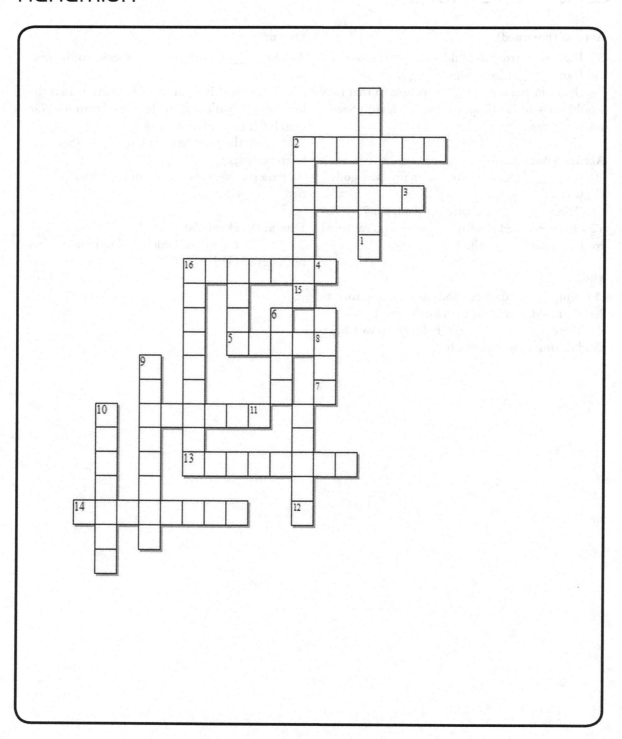

Nehemiah – Questions

Across: (Forward)

2 - The wall was an important_____that surrounded the city. (See reference page).

13 - _____; may have been a priest. ch: 6 (See reference page).

14 - _____; he would later profane the temple through his relationship to Tobiah. ch: 3

Across: (Backwards)

3 - _____; was the brother of Nehemiah. (See reference page).

4 - _____; she was false among the false prophets. ch: 6

8 - Nehemiah gave orders that the people must not_____on the 7th day of the week. ch: 13

11 - Sanballat and_____were enemies of the Jews. ch: 4

Down:

6 - The books of Ezra and Nehemiah are two parts of the_____story. (See reference page).

9 - The book of_____in the Bible tells the story of how Nehemiah and how the people built the walls of Jerusalem. (See reference page).

10 - Most of the people who built the walls were not_____builders. ch: 3

16- _____; Temple servants. ch: 3

Up:

1 - Nehemiah was a very_____man. ch: 5

5 - Nehemiah with the help of_____helped the people to obey God. (See reference page).

7 - Fire had burned the gates of the_____. (See reference page).

12 - Jerusalem was the_____city in Judah. (See reference page).

15 - "_____wives" Nehemiah explained how he had dealt with mixed marriages. ch: 13

Esther

Esther – Questions

Across: (Forward)

4 - Mordecai_____that God had made Esther Queen and that God used her to save the Jews. (See reference page).

5 - King Xerxes said to Queen Esther and Mordecai; I have given to Esther all the_____of Haman. (See reference page).

8 - Haman hated the Jews and he_____to kill them. (See reference page).

Across: (Backwards)

7 - _____' was Esther's uncle. (See reference page).

11 - The book of Esther does not mention the_____of God. (See reference page).

12 - The king allowed the Jews in_____to kill their enemies for two days. (See reference page).

13 - The_____was in front of the king's gate. ch: 4

Down:

1 - Haman was from the family of Agag and his father was_____. ch: 3

3 - The book of Esther uses the_____calendar. ch: 10

9 - The Bible does not mention the book of_____ anywhere else. (See reference page).

10 - _____; je was the king's servant who looked after the king's other wives. ch: 2

Up:

2 - Haman was one of the king's chief_____. (See reference page).

6 - Esther decided to_____Mordecai. ch: 4

14 - _____; was king of the nation called Persia. (See reference page).

15 - The night the king could not_____. ch: 6

Job

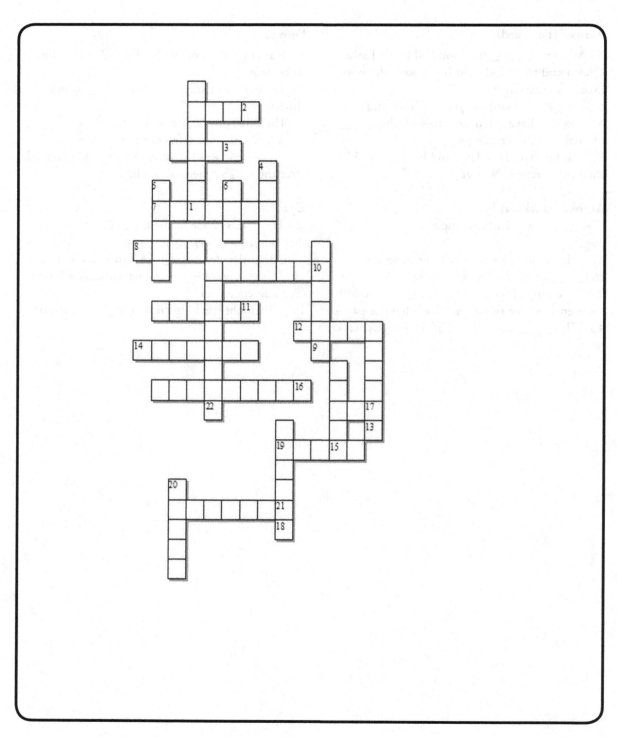

Job - Questions

Across: (Forward)

7 - Job's friends came from three_____. ch: 2

8 - Job's thoughts about a_____gave him hope. ch: 14

12 - The storm sounds like the_____of God. ch: 37

14 - Job wants to_____his troubles with God. ch: 23

19 - _____; was wiser than Job; and told Job not to accuse God. (See reference page).

Across: (Backwards)

2 - Job's own_____, also wanted Job to insult God. ch: 2

3 - Job makes a_____of his troubles. ch: 30

10 - God taught a lesson about the_____. ch: 39

11 - _____; was sure that God is fair and that God would help Job. ch: 8

16 - God was kind to Job even when Job was_____. (See reference page).

17 - The_____of Job's troubles. ch: 42

21 - The devil's name is Satan; it means the_____. ch: 1

Down:

4 - Job's poem about_____. ch: 28

5 - Bildad warns Job not to be_____. ch: 18

6 - God permitted_____to suffer. (See reference page).

20 - Eliphaz described a strange_____. ch: 4

Up:

1 - Job_____God and Job refused to insult God. (See reference page).

9 - _____; only spoke about Job's face; Job had spots all over his body, due to his illness. ch: 11

13 - Job describes his life_____his troubles started. ch: 29

15 - The devil said that God was like a_____ around Job. ch: 3

18 - Elihu spoke like a_____. ch: 32

22 - The devil caused Job's_____. (See reference page).

Psalms – Part One

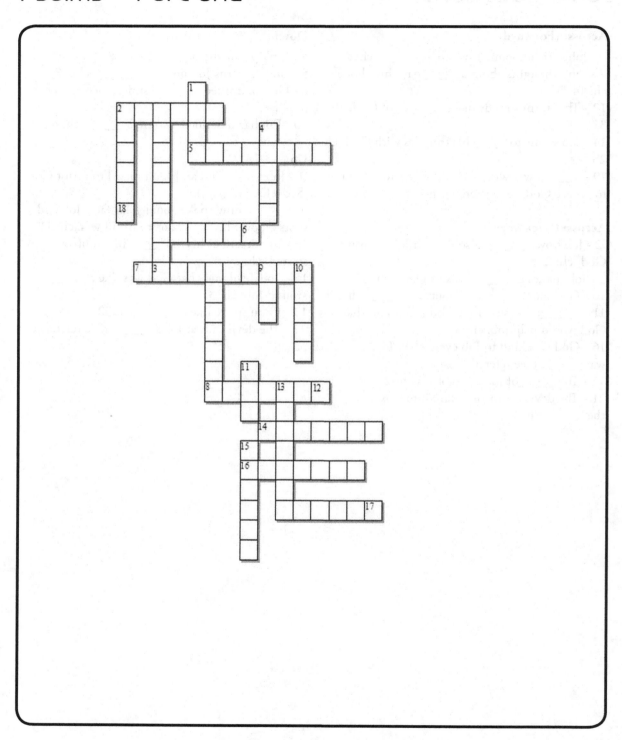

Psalms – Part One – Questions

Across: (Forward)

2 - Some Psalms explain that God will_____us from our troubles. (See reference page).

5 - _____; a place for happy music. Psalms 9, 10.

7 - The book of Psalms is a_____of 150 ancient songs. (See reference page).

14 - David wrote Psalms 3. He wrote it in the_____after he ran away. Psalms 3

16 - _____; more than sweet. Psalms 19

Across: (Backwards)

6 - Many Psalms are glad songs which_____ God. (See reference page).

12 - _____; talks to himself but not very loud. Psalms 1

17 - _____; is "Miktam" in Hebrew. (See reference page).

Down:

1 - _____; is like a wild animal. Psalms 7

4 - King_____wrote many Psalms. (See reference page).

9 - David is very_____. Psalms 6

10 - _____; The Hebrew word for fool. Psalms 14

11 - Some Psalms are_____prayers. (See reference page).

13 - _____; keep safe. Psalms 25

15 - Some Psalms are about the history of_____. (See reference page).

Up:

3 - _____; what is in it pours out. Psalms 23

8 - _____; a special stick that a king held. Psalms 2

18 - Listen to me. In Hebrew it means, "_____ me" Psalms 4

Psalms – Part Two

Psalms – Part Two – Questions

Across: (Forward)

3 - _____; The people that sang in the temple. Psalms 49

8 - _____; the arms of a bird, it uses them to fly. Psalms 36

Across: (Backwards)

1 - _____; Stop and think; pray; make music. Psalms 44

5 - _____; a Psalm that teaches you something. Psalms 42 and 43

9 - _____; when people think that you are bad. Psalms 35

11 - _____; the opposite of Love. Psalms 50

Down:

2 - _____; He wants to be with God in heaven and not with enemies. Psalms 26

4 - I am poor and I need_____Lord. Psalms 40

6 - _____; Illness in the body or mind, because life is difficult. Psalms 31

Up:

7 - The storm came from the_____sea to the mountains of Lebanon. (See reference page).

10 - The Lord is my_____place. Psalms 27

Psalms – Part Three

Psalms –Part Three –Questions

Across: (Forward)

5 - David saw_____bathing and he wanted to have sex with her. Psalms 51

6 - _____; where Jews thought that dead people went. Psalms 55

9 - David went to_____to hide from Saul. Psalms 54

12 - _____; king of Assyria. Psalms 75

13 - _____; listen, and do something. Psalms 64

Across: (Backwards)

2 - _____; does not want to do anything or even live anymore. Psalms 61

8 - Bathsheba was the wife of_____. Psalms 51

Down:

1 - When God decides to be_____. Psalms 75

11 - _____; being sorry for your sins. Psalms 51

Down: (Backwards)

3 - _____; in the Bible it is often a picture of Satan. Psalms 54

7 - When Sennacherib came, people felt as if they were in an_____. Psalms 75

Up:

4 - What men think in their hearts is very_____. (See reference page).

10 - _____; lead an enemy to someone. Psalms 55

Psalms – Part Four

Psalms - Part Four - Questions

Across: (Forward)

2 - _____; being kind when you do not have to be kind. Psalms 77

6 - _____; as a king. (See reference page).

9 - The_____heart; the mind that stops believing in God. Psalms 95

10 - _____; the powerful rulers that have authority. Psalms 90

Across: (Backwards)

4 - _____; two people have agreed what each should do. Psalms 81

7 - _____; another word for festival. Psalms 81

Down:

5 - The Bible uses all three names for God's people; Israel,_____, Joseph. Psalms 80 (See reference page).

8 - _____; Lord, or my Master. Psalms 76

11 - Come to the_____and praise God. Psalms 100

Down: (Backwards)

3 - _____; people who do not obey God; they fight against him. Psalms 82

Up:

1 - _____; God was not furious with his people anymore. Psalms 85

Psalms – Part Five

Psalms – Part Five – Questions

Across: (Forward)

2 - _____; decide who is right and who is wrong. Psalms 122

6 - _____; upright in their hearts. Psalms 125

10 - _____; to say how great someone is. Psalms 117

12 - _____; very large families. Psalms 122

13 - _____; to caress, to love tenderly. Psalms 103

Across: (Backwards)

4 - _____; Jerusalem was on a mountain. Psalms 125

14 - _____; the fruit of a plant; the vine. Psalms 119

15 - _____; special seats that kings sit on. Psalms 122

Down:

3 - _____; is like a bottle made from animal skin. Psalms 119

5 - _____; crooked or perverted. Psalms 101

7 - _____; the mouth that speaks and taste things. Psalms 120

8 - _____; they can hurt me because they are stronger than me. Psalms 119

11 - _____; to test; tested. Psalms 106

Up:

1 - _____; the Lord is great. Psalms 116

9 - _____; very bad. Psalms 125

Psalms – Part Six

Psalms – Part Six – Questions

Across: (Forward)

2 - _____; Ice in rain. Psalms 148

6 - _____; Something you can catch animals or birds with. Psalms 140

11 - David prays that he will not get caught in a_____. Psalms 140

13 - _____; Water that comes on the ground at night. Psalms 133

Across: (Backwards)

8 - _____; Thinks that they are more important than they really are. Psalms 131

9 - _____; Not angry. Psalms 131

14 - _____; A fruit called "The Olive" Psalms 133

15 - "His_____" What he does. Psalms 145

16 - The poison of vipers is on their_____. Psalms 140

Down:

1 - _____; One who says bad things about you that are not true. Psalms 140

3 - "In_____" A bit afraid of someone that you love. Psalms 128

5 - _____; A kind of snake. Psalms 140

10 - _____; Live with God and bring messages from God. Psalms 148

Up:

4 - _____; A short word for mountain. Psalms 150

7 - After the exile, the Jews put 150 Psalms into a_____. (See reference page).

12 - _____; A musical instrument. Psalms 150

17- _____; People could not believe the good thing God was doing for them. Psalms 126

Proverbs

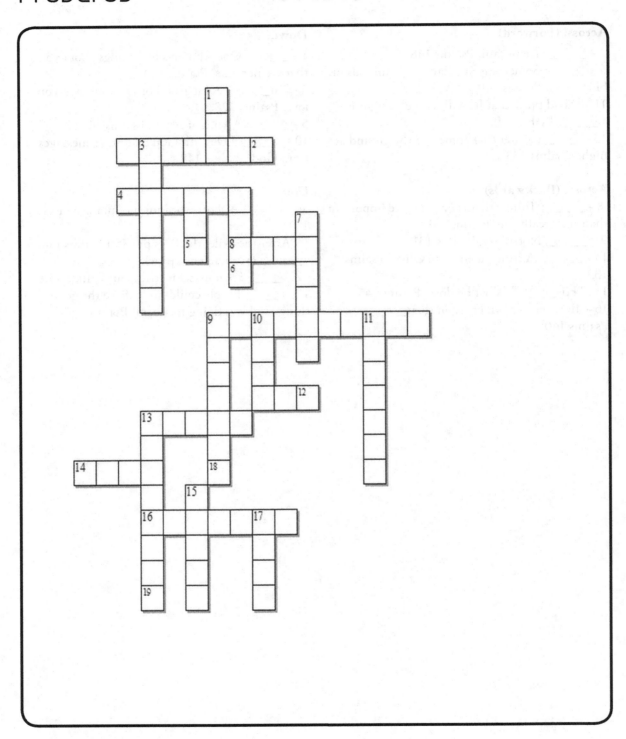

Proverbs - Questions

Across: (Forward)

4 - The book of Proverbs is a collection of articles about_____. (See reference page).

8 - _____; wanted someone to teach him. His own knowledge seemed like nothing, when he thought about God. ch: 30

9 - There is a_____between our own wisdom and God's wisdom. ch: 3

14 - Evil men walk in_____paths. ch: 2

16 - A fool's pride makes him talk too much; his many words will lead him into_____. ch: 14

Across: (Backwards)

2 - The second woman is called "The_____ woman" ch: 9

12 - There is a difference in God's intelligence and_____intelligence. ch: 3

13 - You need to work in the field to grow your_____; without food you will die. ch: 24

Down:

1 - The book of Proverbs tells us about_____ ways. ch: 2

3 - The writer describes a fine house. A house is safe if it's builder is_____. ch: 24

7 - Solomon teaches us that_____are terrible; it encourage people to do evil things. ch: 17

10 - Solomon tells us about_____types of person; The simple, Young people, Wise person and the Intelligent person. ch: 1

11 - It is better to say_____than to speak evil words. ch: 11

15 - The_____called wisdom. ch: 9

17 - Solomon writes about the lazy man. The lazy man tells us that there is a_____outside. ch: 22

Up:

5 - The woman wanted to get the young man in her_____. ch: 7

6 - Solomon is describing a_____; he wants the farmer to be responsible. ch: 27

18 - This chapter is a poem; it has two subjects; a_____woman tempts a man who is not her husband. ch: 5

19 - Solomon compares our_____to a hunter's trap. ch: 6

Ecclesiastes

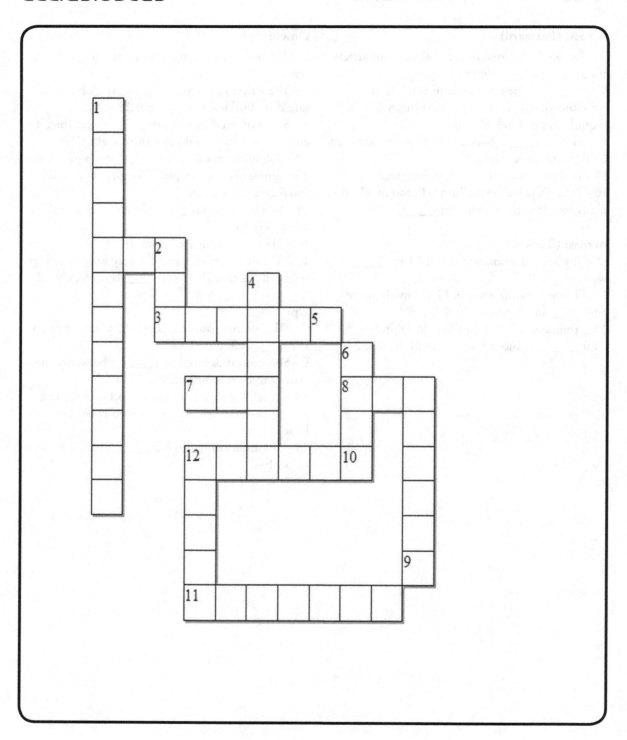

Ecclesiastes - Questions

Across: (Forward)

7 - In the first part of this chapter the writer describes old_____. ch: 12

8 - The teacher was David's_____. ch: 1

11 - The writer calls himself; "The_____" (See reference page).

Across: (Backwards)

2 - There is a time to be born and there is a time to_____. ch: 3

5 - The teacher tells us that_____are not fair to each other. ch: 4

10 - The_____of Ecclesiastes was a king. (See reference page).

Down:

1 - We do not know the name of the person who wrote_____. (See reference page).

4 - The teacher says that we should be_____. ch: 5

6 - It's writer was a very_____man. (See reference page).

12 - The teacher is telling us when something is_____. ch: 3

Up:

3 - The teacher believes that God will be fair in the_____. ch: 8

9 - Things do not always happen as we want them to_____. ch: 9

Song of Solomon

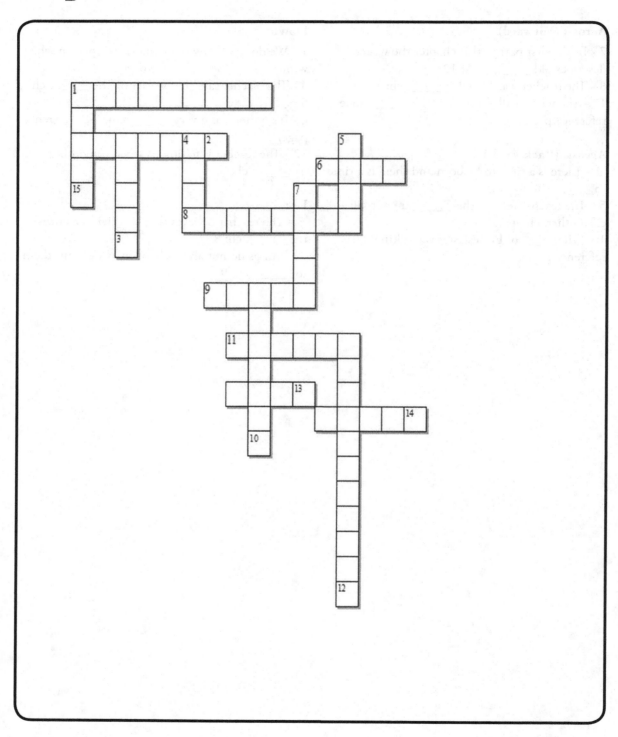

Song of Solomon – Questions

Across: (Forward)

1 - _____; The female form of the name Solomon. (See reference page).

6 - Together, they start to describe a_____picture of their love. ch: 1

8 - _____; A plant. Women used this plant when they wanted to have babies. (See reference page).

9 - This man and woman cared very much about the_____time for their marriage. ch: 2

11 - _____; A woman who has never had sex. (See reference page).

Across: (Backwards)

2 - _____; This country is to the north of Israel where the couple lived. ch: 5

13 - The Song of Solomon is a_____. (See reference page).

14 - The poet calls the people to come to the_____. ch: 3

Down:

4 - _____; A female horse. (See reference page).

5 - The power of_____. ch: 8

7 - _____; The middle part of the body. (See reference page).

Up:

3 - The Song of Solomon is the story of the king and the_____that he loves.)See reference page).

10 - The_____between the young man and the young woman. ch: 6

12 - The_____of the young woman. ch: 7

15 - The Song of Solomon is also called "The Song of_____" (See reference page).

Isaiah

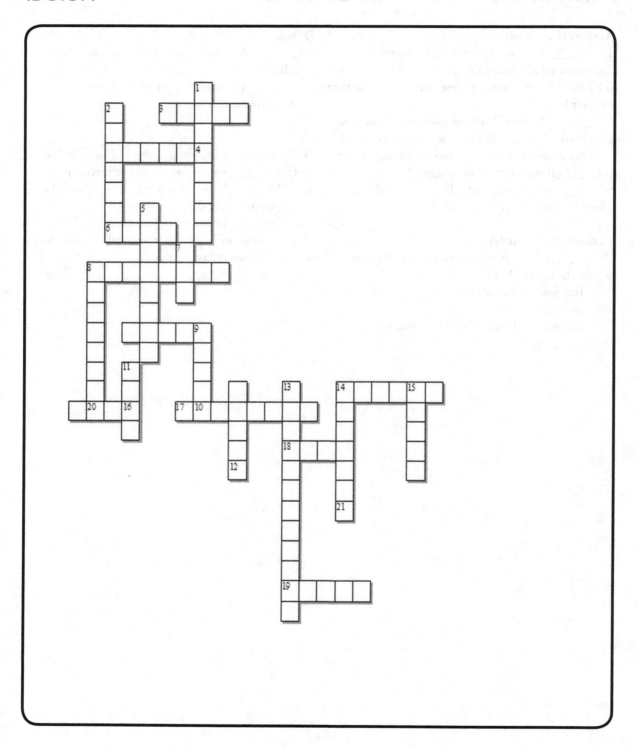

Isaiah - Questions

Across: (Forward)

3 - Isaiah uses the name_____to refer to Egypt. ch: 51

6 - _____; Isaiah's father. (See reference page).

8 - Isaiah uses_____in words to describe how"Total" is the effects of God;s action. ch: 13

14 - Babylonians will take away everything in your_____. ch: 39

17 - _____; God's special people whom he chose. ch: 5

19 - The name Isaiah means "God_____" (See reference page).

Across: (Backwards)

4 - _____; He was king of Judah for over 50 years. ch: 6

9 - _____; Any agent that God will use to kill. ch: 31

16 - _____; Get up to act. ch: 60

18 - Isaiah's fierce_____was like the pain of a woman who is giving birth to a baby. ch: 21

Down:

1 - For my_____are not your thoughts. ch: 55

2 - _____; Father of a crowd. ch: 51

5 - The names; Israel, Ephraim, Samaria, all refer to the_____half of the land. ch: 7

7 - The Lord's "Strong_____" is a picture phrase for his power to do things. ch: 52

11 - _____; King of Israel. Selected a hill for a new capital; Samaria. ch: 28 (See reference page).

13 - _____; Substance to burn for a sweet smell; to give honour to God or to a false god. (See reference page).

15 - Isaiah wrote about a_____who would have no human father. (See reference page).

Up:

10 - Isaiah laughs; A foolish people who are serious about_____. ch: 44

12 - But they that wait upon the Lord shall_____ their strength; ch: 40

20 - Chapters 7 through 12 refer to the need to trust in God and not in_____. ch: 7

21 - Isaiah was a_____. (See reference page).

Jeremiah

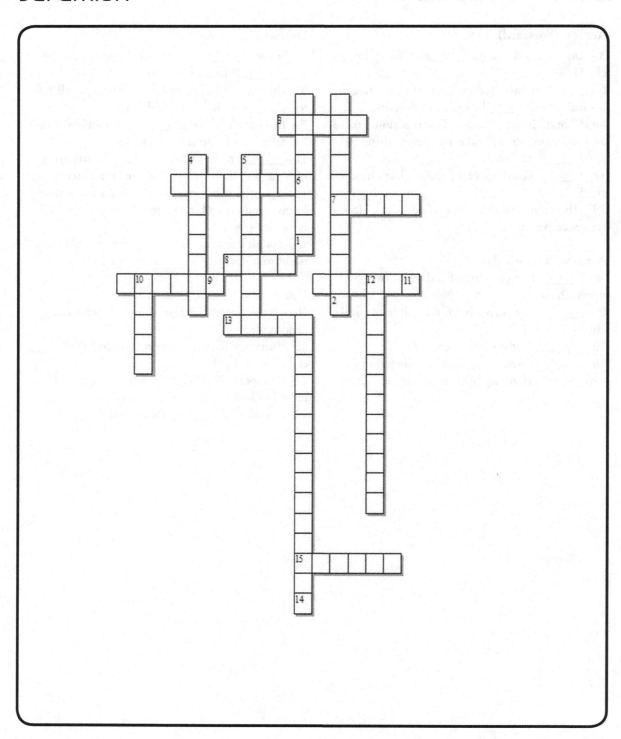

Jeremiah – Questions

Across: (Forward)

3 - I have put my words in thy_____. ch: 1

7 - Be not afraid of their_____. ch: 1

8 - But his word was in mine heart as burning_____shut up in my bones. ch: 20

13 - _____; Vaulted rooms. Not a nice place. ch: 37

15 - _____; Not the husband of Bathsheba. He echoed the warning of Jeremiah. ch: 26

Across: (Backwards)

6 - _____; The son Hezekiah king of Judah. ch: 15

9 - _____; Jeremiah's companion and stenographer. ch: 43

11 - _____; other gods. ch: 2

Down:

4 - _____; he was born into the priesthood. (See reference page).

5 - _____; To call; Alluding to it's cry. ch: 17

10 - I cannot speak: for I am a_____. ch: 1

12 - _____; Many idols. ch: 4

Up:

1 - _____; A poisonous plant. ch: 23

2 - _____; The first or choice part of the harvest of salvation. ch: 2

14 - _____; Because they chose deception. ch: 6

Lamentations

Lamentations - Questions

Across: (Forward)

5 - The_____speaks on behalf of God's people. ch: 3

7 - The old men have_____sitting at the city's gate. ch: 5

9 - _____; They now walk over the stones. ch: 5

Across: (Backwards)

2 - The city gates are silent_____. ch: 1

3 - The writer is talking about the bad things that the enemy has done to the women in_____. ch: 3

6 - _____; Is a way to talk about the strength of Israel. ch: 2

Down:

1 - _____; He was the last king of Judah. ch: 4 (See reference page).

4 - _____Wrote the book of Lamentations. (See reference page).

Up:

8 - The children were_____for them in the bad times of my people. ch: 4 (See reference page).

10- Lamentations is a book of_____poems. (See reference page).

11 - Jerusalem's people are speaking as if the city were a_____. ch: 1

Ezekiel

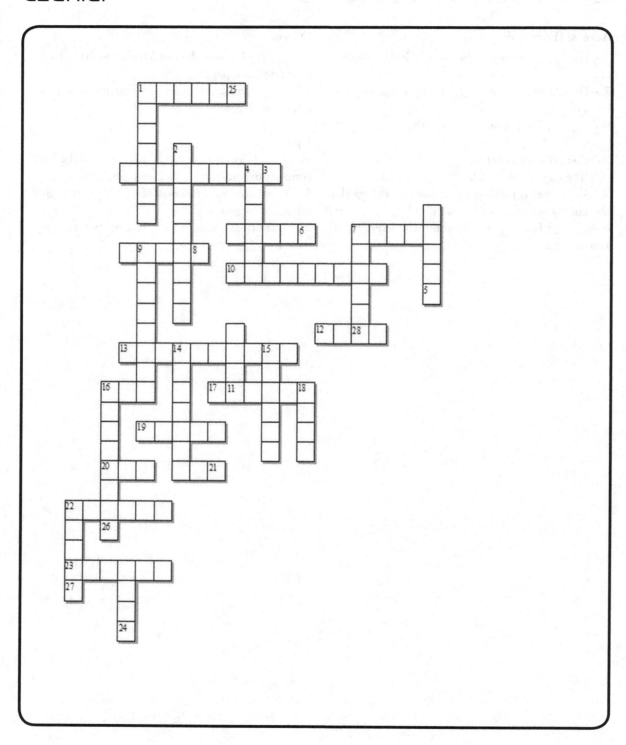

Ezekiel - Questions

Across: (Forward)

7 - _____; Six cubits in diameter, the thickness of the walls. ch: 41

10 - _____; Concubines, the Egyptians princes are described as having unpleasant characteristics. ch: 23

12 - In the vision Ezekiel records the stormy_____. ch: 1

13 - _____; Appealing to the wisdom of his gods; but the God of heaven was in control. ch: 21

16 - _____; A town thought to be 25 miles south of Port Said, on the Suez canal. *See reference page).

17 - Ezekiel eats the_____. ch: 3

19 - _____; and fire over the city. ch: 10

20 - God showed Ezekiel a picture of a_____ temple. (See reference page).

22 - God showed Ezekiel events that would happen in the_____. (See reference page).

23 - Each wheel seemed to have a wheel_____a wheel. ch: 1

Across: (Backwards)

3 - The_____had four wings each. ch: 1

6 - All the_____reflected the glory of God. ch: 1

8 - Ezekiel belong to the family of_____. (See reference page).

21 - The_____moves with a force that nobody cas oppse. ch: 1

25 - Ezekiel saw something that was like a_____. ch: 1

Down:

1 - _____; Was a prophet. (See reference page).

2 - _____; is like Samaria and Sodom. ch: 16

4 - The two eagles; The king of Babylon; The second eagle, king of Egypt_____. ch: 17

9 - _____; Something lifted up. ch: 45

14 - _____; The Greek name for Edom. ch: 35

15 - _____; The literal meaning, of the name is "her own tabernacle (tent)" ch: 23

18 - Ezekiel is to be a_____out for the people. ch: 3

Up:

5 - God will break the_____gods. ch: 6

11 - Ezekiel_____and divides his hair. ch: 5

24 - Ezekiel was a priest, the son of_____the priest. (See reference page).

Up: (Backwards)

26 - Ezekiel means, "God gives_____" (See reference page).

27 - A vine without_____. ch: 15

28 - On the throne there was a_____. ch: 1

Daniel

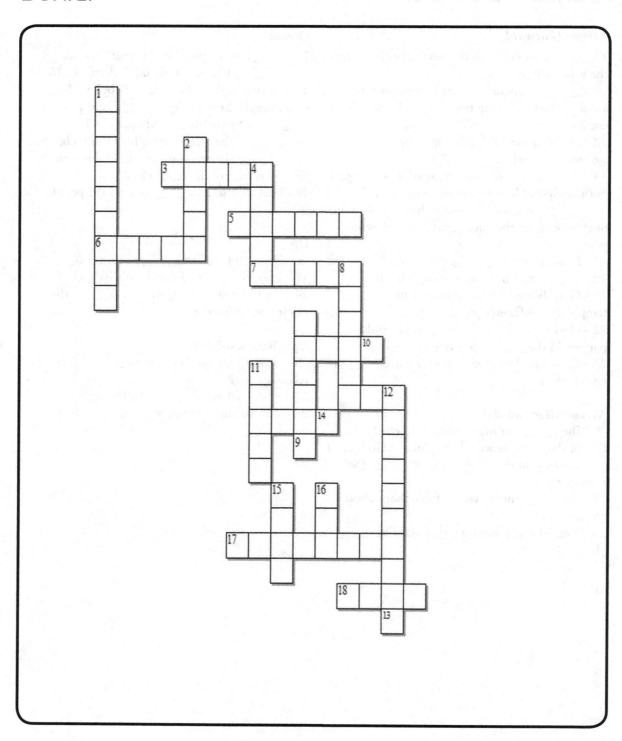

Daniel - Questions

Across: (Forward)

3 - The man wore_____clothes and a gold belt. ch: 10

5 - _____; He was one of the king's chief officials. ch: 2

6 - In the dream the king had seen a large_____; it was in four parts. ch: 2

7 - Gabriel told Daniel that God had other plans. His plans were for a period of 70_____7 years. ch: 9

17 - Daniel saw four animals. There would be four powerful_____. ch: 7

18 - In the dream he saw a_____; The tree tall and it grew taller. ch: 3

Across: (Backwards)

10 - Daniel saw a male_____with a large horn. ch: 8

12 - Nebuchadnezzar was so angry that his face went_____. ch: 3

14 - The Bible introduces us to_____of these young men. ch: 1

Down:

1 - The young men received the best_____. ch: 1

2 - Nebuchadnezzar_____the best of the young men from the people that he had defeated. ch: 1

4 - Did we not tie up_____men and throw them into the fire? ch: 3

8 - The_____part of the book of Daniel tells about Daniel's dreams. (See reference page).

11 - The_____part of the book of Daniel in the Bible tell some stories from the life of Daniel and his friends. (see reference page).

15 - Nebuchadnezzar had to eat grass; his hair and nails grew_____. ch: 4

16 - Shadrach, Meshach and Abednego thought they might die because they were loyal to_____. ch: 3

Up:

9 - The_____man was Jesus; The Son of the real God. ch: 3

13 - _____; He drank from the gold and silver cups that belonged to God. ch: 5

Hosea

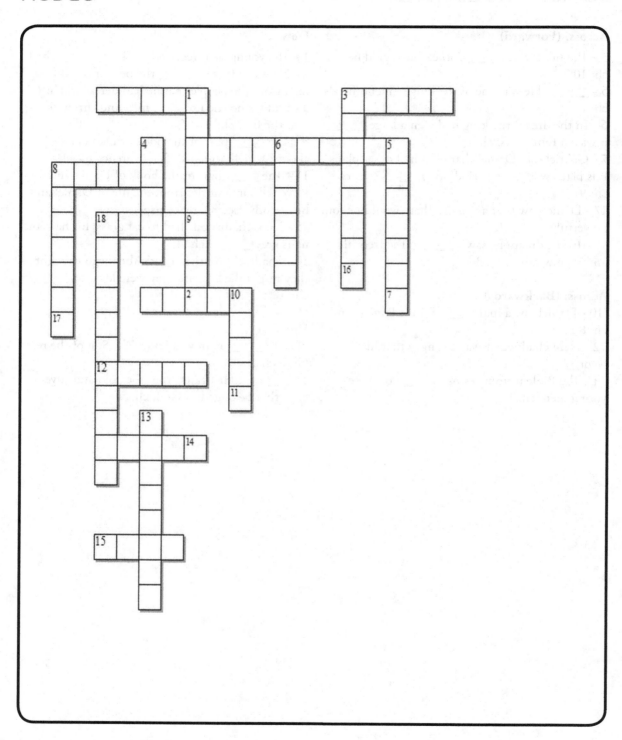

Hosea - Questions

Across: (Forward)

3 - God told Hosea to_____a wife who was not loyal to him. (See reference page).

8 - Hosea says, God is like a_____. ch: 2

12 - _____; is a mountain. ch: 5

15 - He shall_____like a lion. ch: 11

Across: (Backwards)

1 - Hosea uses a picture of a_____; large oven, burnt bread, sleep. ch: 7

5 - _____; An ordinary prostitute. (See reference page).

9 - The Israelites will destroy themselves with_____. ch: 8

10 - Everything in the book of_____is a message from God. Ch: 1

14 - _____; A place where Israel made sacrifices. ch: 3

Down:

6 - The people of_____were good at fighting wars. (See reference page).

13 - The_____at Sinai. (See reference page).

18 - _____; is a metaphor. ch: 12

Up:

4 - _____; The wife of Hosea. ch: 1

16 - The book only mentions one king; his name is_____. ch: 1

Up: (Backwards)

2 - The curses and_____of Hosea are connected to the covenant. (See reference page).

7 - The_____also were earning money at the sacrifices. 4

11 - _____; Being true to a covenant. ch: 2

17 - _____; God sows. ch: 1

Joel

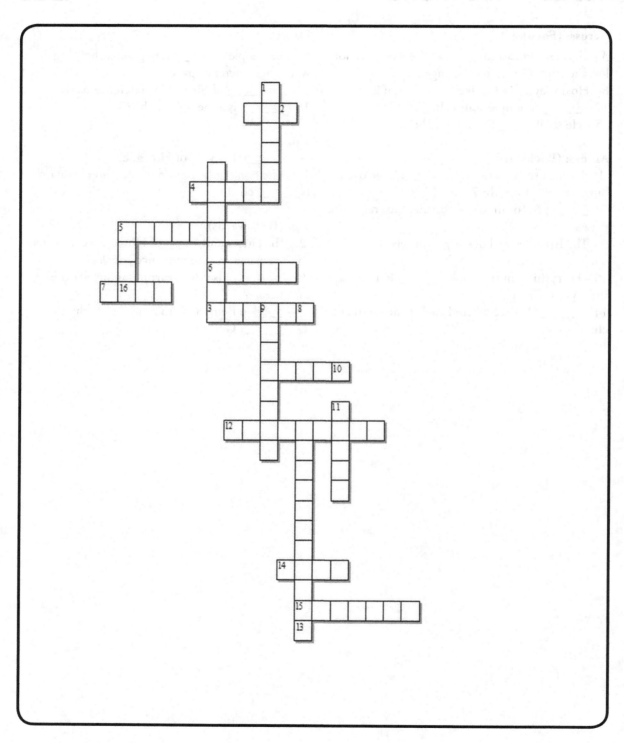

Joel – Questions

Across: (Forward)

4 - I will give back to you the_____the locusts have eaten. ch: 2

5 - _____; Eat all the plants in Israel. ch: 1

6 - _____; A fruit that people make a drink from. ch: 3

7 - The land in front of them is like the garden of_____. ch: 2

12 - At that time new wine will come from the_____. ch: 3

14 - _____; Tells the people that they should love God. (See reference page).

15 - Joel says, the_____have done great things. ch: 2

Across: (Backwards)

2 - The seeds under the earth are_____. ch: 1

8 - Joel tells people to_____. ch: 1

10 - The cows make a sad_____. ch: 1

Down:

1 - Wake up you_____. ch: 1

9 - The day of the Lord is_____. ch: 2

11 - Old people should be_____than young people. ch: 1

Up:

3 - Locusts run_____as an army runs into a fight. ch: 2

13 - _____; The valley of decision.. ch: 3

Up: (Backwards)

16- Joel tells the people about a new day; "The day of the_____" (See reference page).

Amos

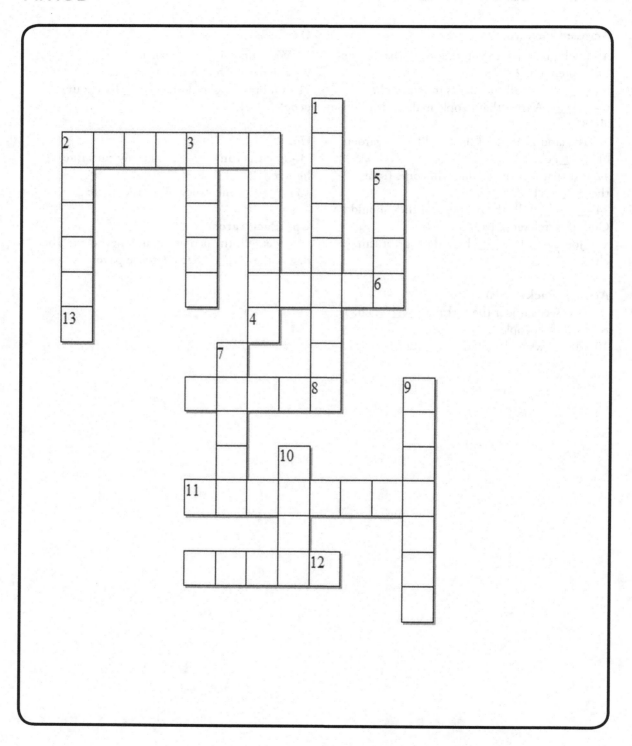

Amos - Questions

Across: (Forward)

2 - Amos was not a_____. (See reference page).

11 - _____; The capital of Aram. ch: 1

Across: (Backwards)

6 - Amos looks to the future; He looks beyond the_____. ch: 9

8 - Amos looked after_____. (See reference page).

12 - God will_____the good times in Israel to end. ch: 6

Down:

1 - Amos ask the people from Ashdod and Egypt to look at their own_____. ch: 3

3 - Amos uses pictures to send a message to Israel. A_____cart on very wet ground. ch: 2

5 - Amos reminds the people about God's word; We find_____life as we look for God and obey his laws. ch: 5

7 - Amos came from_____, about 12 miles south of Jerusalem. (See reference page).

9 - Amos is probably a short name for_____. (See reference page).

10 - _____; It was a Philistine city; between Egypt and Israel. ch: 1

Up:

4 - A plumb line; A piece of string with a_____ on the end. ch: 7

Up: (Backwards)

13 - Amos was angry with Edom's_____. ch: 1

Obadiah

Obadiah - Questions

Across: (Forward)

7 - Third prophecy; The day of_____. ch: 1

Across: (Backwards)

2 - _____; The servant of Yahweh. (See reference page).

6 - Second prophecy; People steal things; They are not_____. ch: 1

8 - God punished the people from Edom for their_____deeds. (See reference page).

Down:

1 - Edon's people thought that they were_____ than other nations. ch: 1

3 - First prophecy; Pride brings_____. ch: 1

4 - Obadiah is the_____book in the Old Testament. (See reference page).

Up:

5 - Edom. The people that were from Esau's_____. ch: 1

Up: (Backwards)

9 - The book of Obadiah is a short message about the country of_____. (See reference page).

Jonah

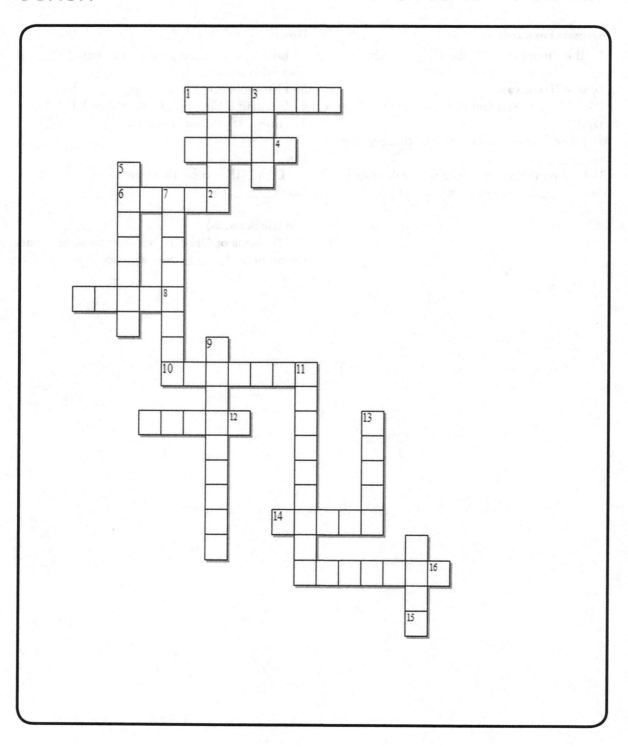

Jonah - Questions

Across: (Forward)

1 - Jonah did not drown; God caused a large whale (fish) to_____him. (See reference page).

6 - Jonah is wrong and God is_____. ch: 4
).

10 - The_____on the ship knew that Jonah believed in God; They ask Jonah to pray to God. ch: 1

14 - The whale (fish) threw Jonah out of it's_____ onto the land. ch: 2

Across: (Backwards)

4 - Jonah was fully aware that God caused the_____ while the ship was in the sea. (See reference page).

8 - Nineveh was an_____of Jonah's country Israel. (See reference page

12 - Jonah went down to the port of_____. ch: 1

16 - God sent Jonah to_____. (See reference page).

Down:

3 - _____; A set of objects by which to choose something by chance. (See reference page).

5 - Jonah was a_____. (See reference page).

9 - Jonah knew that he had_____God. ch: 3

11 - _____; A dress of very rough material. (See reference page).

13 - God caused the whale (fish) to return_____to the dry land. (See reference page).

Down:(Backwards)

7 - The storm came when Jonah was_____on the ship. ch: 1

Up:

2 - The sailors_____Jonah into the sea. ch: 1

15 - Jonah tried to escape God. He tried to travel elsewhere by_____. (See reference page).

Micah

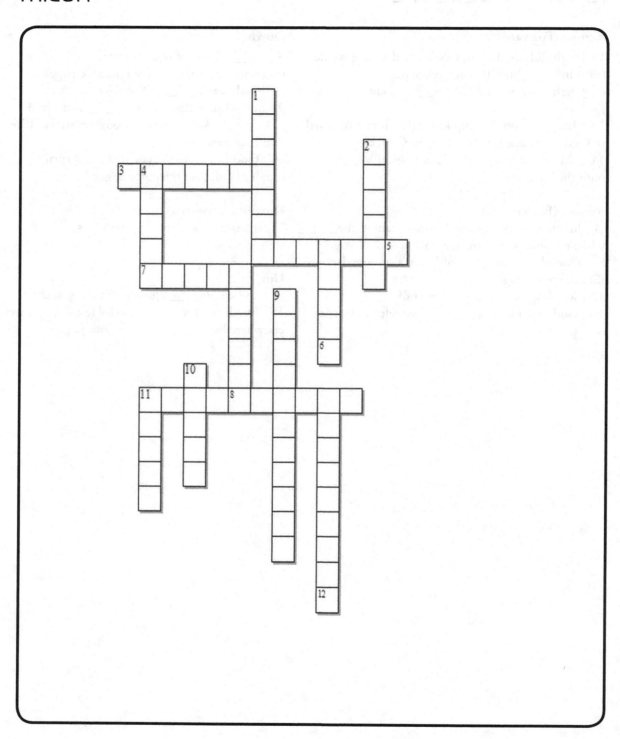

Micah – Questions

Across: (Forward)

3 - _____; Imagery, drawn from birth pain. ch: 4

7 - Micah was one of the 12_____prophets. (See reference page).

11 - Micah is called the_____. (See reference page).

Across: (Backwards)

5 - The_____came to Micah with great power. ch: 1

Down:

1 - Micah was an inhabitant of Moresheth Gath, a small_____. (See reference page).

2 - Micah's name means "Who is like_____" (See reference page).

9 - And thou shalt have no more_____. ch: 5

10 - _____; Thorns. ch: 7

11 - _____; was the 6th in order of the minor prophets. (See reference page).

Down: (Backwards)

4 - "_____prophets" They wrote shorter prophecies than the 4 greater prophets. (See reference page).

Up:

6 - Micah_____; He has seen what will happen to Samaria. ch: 1

8 - Evil leader and false prophets will_____. chL 2

12 - _____; your behavior needs to be judged and punished. ch: 3

Nahum

Nahum - Questions

Across: (Forward)

1 - _____; The main city in Assyria. ch: 1

6 - Keep the munition. Guard the_____place. ch: 2

9 - _____; God controls nature. ch: 1

Across: (Backwards)

5 - _____; To regard; The boasting of the Assyrians would work against them. ch: 1

11 - _____; God cares about his children. ch: 1

Down:

2 - _____; God does not punish out of development of hatred. ch: 1

3 - _____; Molten. This may have been the name of the Queen from the Hebrew root, "stand by" Stand by the king. ch: 2

8 - _____; The opposite of restorer. ch: 2

Up:

4 - _____; That is, weak. ch: 3

7 - _____; Or noise. The fall of the wicked city. ch: 3

10 - _____; Spiritual unfaithfulness. ch: 3

12 - Hebrew was the language that_____spoke. (See reference page).

Habakkuk

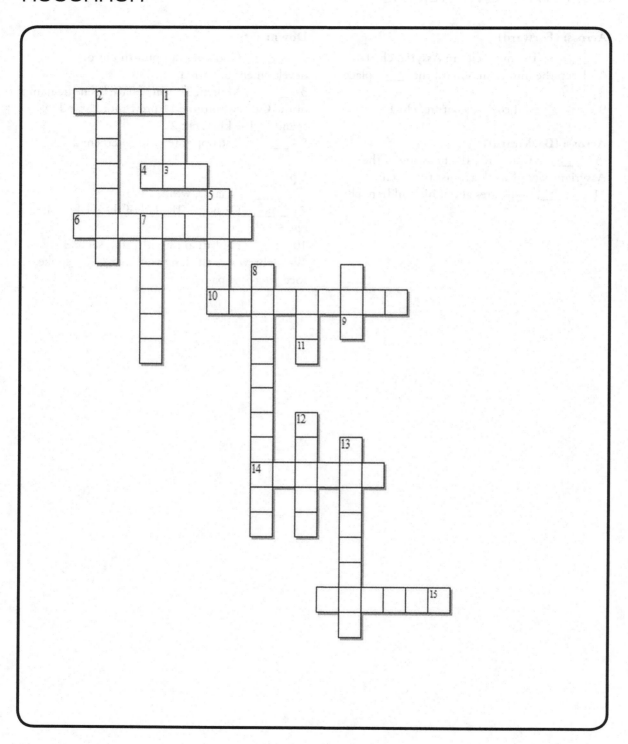

Habakkuk - Questions

Across: (Forward)

4 - Habakkuk is writing about his_____country. ch: 1

6 - _____; An indication of judgement. (See reference page).

10 - _____; The major ethnic group in Babylon. (See reference page).

14 - The_____is called a deer. ch: 3

Across: (Backwards)

1 - God brought his people out of_____. ch: 3

15 - The book of Habakkuk ends with a Psalms (song), "God will_____his people. (See reference page).

Down:

2 - Habakkuk was a_____. ch: 1

7 - Habakkuk ask God, why God's people must_____. (See reference page).

8 - The_____have false gods. ch: 1

12 - Habakkuk complained_____to God. (See reference page).

13 - _____; He who holds somebody close to him. (See reference page).

Down:(Backwards)

5 - Habakkuk ask God why_____people succeed. (See reference page).

Up:

3 - _____; will destroy Babylon. ch: 2

9 - "_____people" Rob other people, are not honest, kill people, many become drunks, have false gods. ch: 2

11 - God brought his people through the_____ sea. ch: 3

Zephaniah

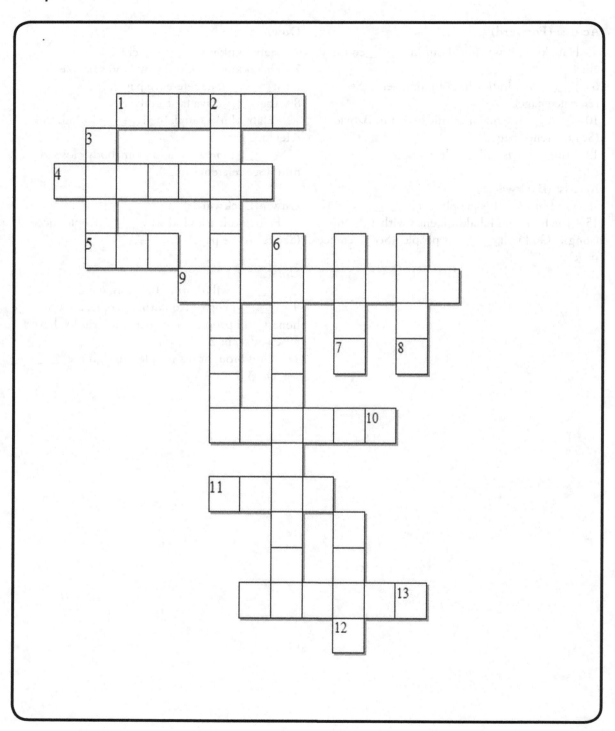

Zephaniah – Questions

Across: (Forward)

1 - _____; Pictures of a depopulated Nineveh. ch: 2

4 - Which fill their_____houses with violence and deceit. ch: 1

5 - Zephaniah says, people must confess their evil deeds to_____. (See reference page).

9 - _____; was a prophet. (See reference page).

11 - Therefore_____ye upon me, saith the Lord. ch: 3

Across: (Backwards)

10 - _____; Rebellious. ch: 3

13 - Zephaniah explained that God would_____ many countries because of their evil deeds. (See reference page).

Down:

2 - _____; Securely, undisturbed. ch: 2

6 - _____; A portion of the Philistines supposed by many to have originated in Crete. ch: 2

Down: (Backwards)

3 - God loves them and God will make them_____. (See reference page).

Up:

7 - For the day of the Lord is at_____. ch: 1

8 - _____; Cut off. He never belonged there. ch: 1

12 - At that time I will_____all that afflict thee. ch: 3

Haggai

Haggai - Questions

Across: (Forward)

2 - And I will overthrow the_____. ch: 2

4 - _____; No rain, the cattle died. ch: 1

5 - And will make thee as a_____. ch: 2

7 - I will_____heavens and the earth. ch: 2

Across: (Backwards)

8 - Is it not in your_____in comparison of it as nothing? ch: 2

9 - Is the seed yet in the_____? ch: 2

Down:

1 - And I will fill this house with_____. ch: 2

Up:

3 - And he that earneth wages earneth wages to put to put it into a bag with_____. ch: 1

6 - Haggai was a_____. (See reference page).

10 - Haggai told the people that they should_____God's temple. (See reference page).

Zechariah

Zechariah - Questions

Across: (Forward)

3 - Zechariah was a_____. (See reference page).

5 - The man on a red_____. ch: 1

7 - _____; Those who pretended to reveal the will of the gods. ch: 10

13 - _____; A combination of two Syrian towns. ch: 12

Across: (Backwards)

4 - As Zachariah became older he thought about the_____. (See reference page).

9 - _____; To tell people what God is saying. (See reference page).

11 - The man who was measuring_____. ch: 2

14 - The_____chariots. ch: 6

15 - _____; The place of judgement in a city. ch: 8

16 - The flying_____. ch: 5

17 - _____; Something that a prophet sees. ch: 1

18 - _____; Born out of wedlock or of alien birth. ch: 9

Down:

1 - _____; write some things about Jesus. (See reference page).

2 - _____; and olive tree. ch: 4

8 - Zachariah begins his book with a short_____. (See reference page).

Up:

6 - Zachariah means, "God_____" (See reference page).

10 - The_____priest has returned to Jerusalem. ch: 3

12 - _____; The transportation system was being destroyed. ch: 14

16 - The woman in a_____. ch: 5

Up: (Backwards)

19 - The four_____. ch: 1

Malachi

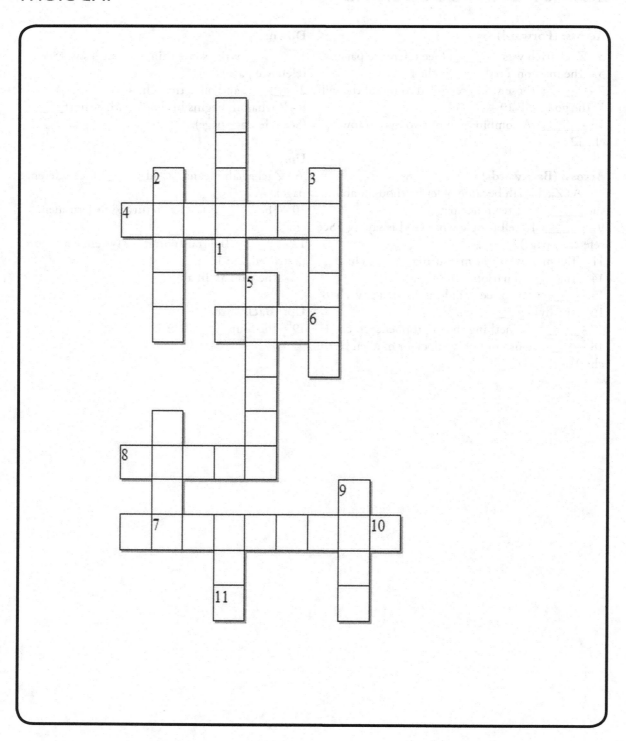

Malachi - Questions

Across: (Forward)

4 - _____; It is the last book in the Bible's Old Testament. (See reference page).

8 - Who is there even among you that would shut the_____for naught? ch: 1

Across: (Backwards)

6 - "Hated_____" Refused the merciful love of God. ch: 1

10 - Malachi is a name that means "My_____" (See reference page).

Down:

2 - _____; In the Hebrew language it means "cheat" ch: 3

3 - Bring ye all the_____into the storehouse; ch: 3

5 - _____; Our freedom at the time of Christ's appearance. ch: 4

9 - _____; God speaks about him as one man; He was a cruel man. ch: 2

Up:

1 - _____; Another name for Israel. ch: 2

7 - _____; The people or land of Esau. ch: 1

11 - _____; Not to obey God. ch: 2

Matthew

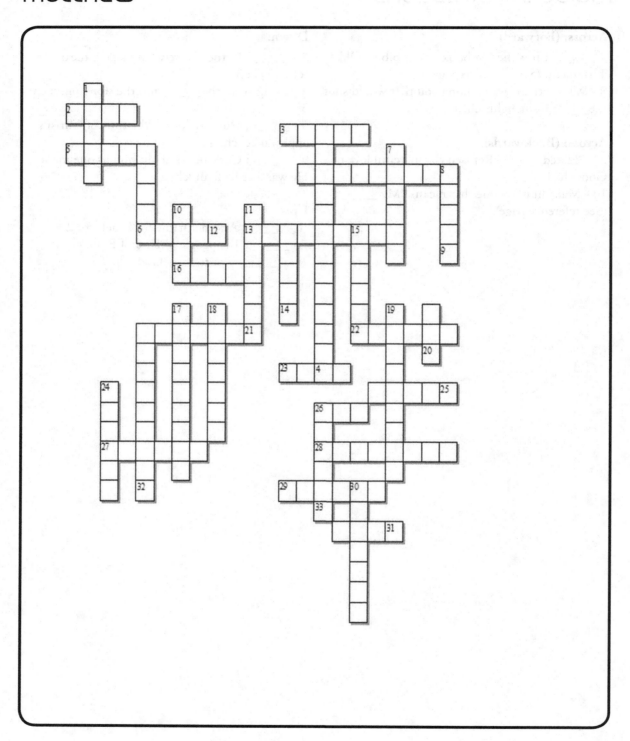

Matthew – Questions

Across: (Forward)

2 - Thou shalt_____the Lord thy God with all thy heart. ch: 22

3 - Matthew explains that_____cured many ill people. (See reference page).

5 - Jesus_____5000 people. ch: 14

13 - What the pharisees and_____taught. ch: 16

16 - Matthew includes a speech by Jesus called "The sermon on the_____" (See reference page).

22 - Matthew introduces the Lord's_____. ch: 6

23 - Matthew uses much of what_____wrote. (See reference page).

26 - Jesus was Mary's_____. ch: 1

27 - Matthew's_____is a book about Jesus' life. (See reference page).

28 - _____; One of a group of Jews who thought that they obeyed all God's rules. ch: 9

29 - Give to Caesar what belongs to_____. ch: 22

Across: (Backwards)

8 - Jesus was born in a town called_____. ch: 2

12 - Matthew did not write the_____book about Jesus. (See reference page).

21 - The work of John the_____. ch: 3

25 - Matthew collected_____. (See reference page).

31 - _____; wrote about Jesus first. (See reference page).

Down:

1 - Jesus has_____over evil spirits. ch: 12

7 - Jesus is the_____. ch: 1

17 - Jesus chooses the first_____. ch: 4

18 - Matthew became one of Jesus' 12_____ friends. (See reference page).

19 - The Jewish Government was called the_____. ch: 26

24 - Matthew wrote about the things that Jesus_____. (See reference page).

30 - Jesus is also the son of_____. ch: 1

Down: (Backwards)

10 - Very early on Sunday morning the two women called_____came to the grave. ch: 28

11 - The_____of Jesus. ch: 3

15 - Jesus feeds 4000_____. ch: 15

Up: (Backwards)

9 - The_____of Jesus. ch: 1

33 - The Lord's_____. ch: 26

Up:

4 - But seek ye first the kingdom of God and his_____; ch: 6

6 - The devil_____Jesus. ch: 4

14 - Bethlehem means House of_____. ch: 2

20 - The story about the_____young women. ch: 25

32 - The Christian church put Matthew's book first because Matthew often refers to the Old_____. (See reference page).

Mark

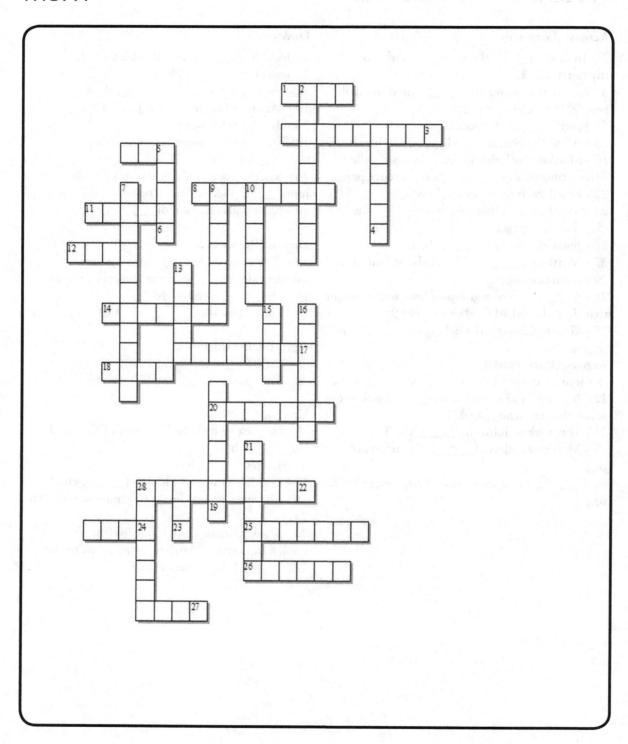

Mark - Questions

Across: (Forward)

1 - _____; Aramaic word for father. (See reference page).

8 - The_____of Jairus. ch: 5: verses 35-43.

11 - Mark shows that Jesus was also_____. (See reference page).

12 - The Gospel explains how Jesus came back to_____again. (See reference page).

14 - Mark has written about Jesus' popularity in_____. ch: 2

18 - The_____to kill Jesus. ch: 14: verses 1-2.

20 - Jesus_____12 Apostles. ch: 3: verses 13-19.

25 - Mark explains in chapter 6: verses 17-18 why Herod_____put John in prison. ch: 1

26 - _____; was Simon's brother. ch: 3

Across: (Backwards)

3 - The_____was John the Baptist. ch: 1

5 - Mark wanted to show that Jesus was the_____of God. (See reference page).

17 - Mark was a relative of_____. (See reference page).

22 - _____; and Spiritually blind people. ch: 8: verses 14-26.

24 - The name" Peter" means_____. ch: 3

27 - Jesus cures the mother of Peter's_____. ch: 1: verses 29-31.

Down:

2 - _____; Was the name of a false god. ch: 3

7 - Mark uses the word_____several times in his writings. (See reference page).

9 - One of the 12 special men that Jesus sent out. (See reference page).

10 - _____; A book that describes the life and death of Jesus. (See reference page).

13 - Jesus_____on water. ch: 6: verses 45-52.

15 - _____; He was the first person to write a Gospel. (See reference page).

16 - James and John were the sons of_____. ch: 10: verses 35-40.

28 - Jesus explains the_____. ch: 4

Down: (Backwards)

21 - Mark recorded some of the actual_____ words that Jesus used. (See reference page).

Up:

4 - Peter_____Jesus. ch: 14: verses 66-72.

19 - Jesus teaches about marriage and_____. ch: 10

23 - Jesus cures a_____with an Evil spirit. ch: 9: verses 14-29.

Up: (Backwards)

6 - There is a heavy_____at the entrance of the rock grave. ch: 16

Luke

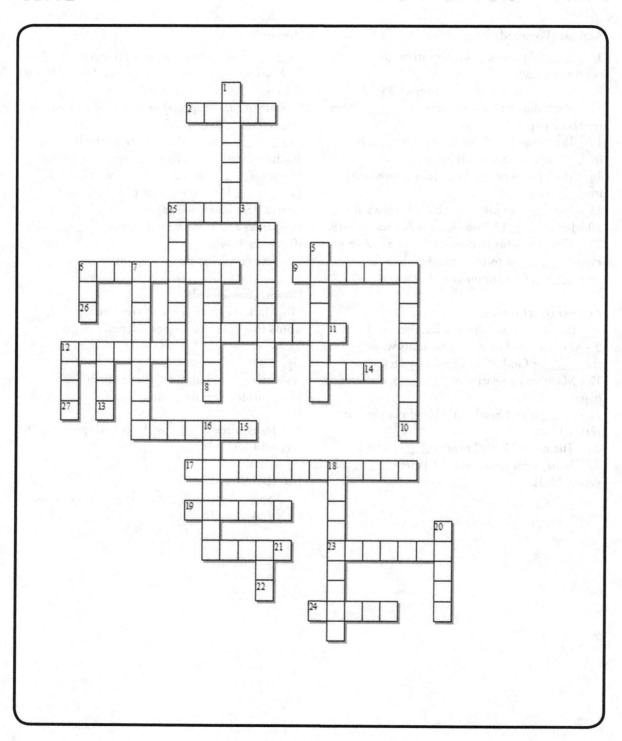

Luke - Questions

Across: (Forward)

2 - Luke emphasise that Jesus had come for the_____world. ch: 3: verses 3-17.

6 - Jesus sends out more_____. ch: 10: verses 1-12.

9 - The rich man and_____. ch: 16: verses 19-31.

12 - The parable of the_____seed. ch: 13: verses 18-19.

17 - He hath sent me to heal the_____. ch: 4:

19 - _____; examines Jesus. ch: 23: verses 1-7.

23 - Luke came from_____. (See reference page).

24 - Luke's Gospel tells the story of the life and work of_____. (See reference page).

Across: (Backwards)

3 - And shalt call his name_____. ch: 1

11 - The parable of the friend at_____. ch: 11: verses 5-8.

14 - _____; was a doctor. (See reference page).

15 - The_____spirit. ch: 11: verses 24-26.

21 - The parable of the man who_____grain. ch: 8: verses 4-8.

Down:

1 - Father_____them for they know not what they do. ch: 23: verses 32-43.

4 - The widow's_____. ch: 21: verses 1-4.

5 - John_____Jesus. ch: 3: verses 21-22.

7 - Luke was often Paul's_____in his travels. (See reference page).

16 - He was parted from them and was_____up into heaven. ch: 24: verses 50-53.

18 - Joseph and_____buries Jesus. ch: 23: verses 50-56.

20 - The babe leaped in her womb and Elisabeth was filled with the Holy_____. ch: 1

25- The_____and the Angels. ch: 2: verses 8-20.

Up:

8 - Luke was a_____. (See reference page).

10 - _____; Was the head of the tax district of Jericho. ch: 19: verses 1-10.

13 - Luke's second book_____continues the story after Jesus went back to heaven. (See reference page).

22 - Luke wrote_____books of the New Testament. (See reference page).

26 - And behold thy cousin Elisabeth, she hath also conceived a son in her_____age; ch: 1

Up: (Backwards)

27 - And the Angel said unto her, fear not,_____; ch: 1

John

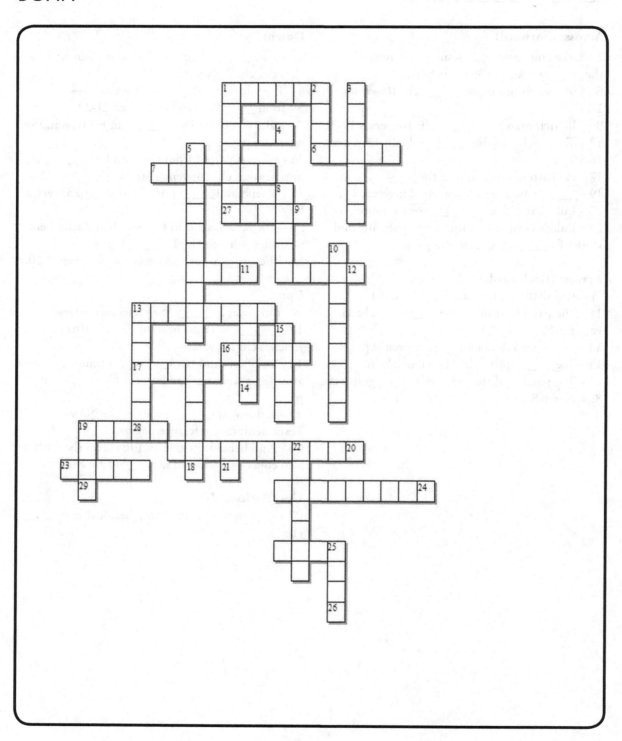

John - Questions

Across: (Forward)

1 - The_____argue about Jesus. ch: 7: verses 40-44.

6 - Jesus_____. ch: 11: verses 26-37.

7 - The Roman soldiers_____Jesus. ch: 19: verses 17-27.

13 - John only recorded 7_____which he called "signs" (See reference page).

16 - John had a brother called_____. (See reference page).

17 - But that the world through him might be_____; ch: 3:

19 - Jesus is the_____for the world. ch: 8: verses 12-20.

Across: (Backwards)

4 - Peter, James and_____, were Jesus' special friends. (See reference page).

9 - _____; Betrays Jesus. ch: 18: verses 1-11.

11 - _____; Who has always existed. ch: 1: verses 1-5.

12 - _____peter says that he does not know Jesus. ch: 18: verses 15-18.

20 - _____; And Nathanael refer unto the same person. ch: 1: (See reference page).

23 - Blood and_____flows from Jesus' body. ch: 19: verses 31-37.

24 - _____; Saith unto him, how can a man be born when he is old? ch: 3:

25 - Mary pours expensive perfume over Jesus'_____. ch: 12: verses 1-11.

Down:

3 - _____; John's father. (See reference page).

5 - I am the true vine and my father is the_____. ch: 15:

8 - John also established that Jesus was))))). (See reference page).

10 - Joseph from Arimathea and_____put Jesus' body in a grave. ch: 19: verses 38-42.

15 - _____; is completely human and completely God. (See reference page).

22 - Jesus called John and James "The sons of_____" (See reference page).

Down: (Backwards)

2 - Jesus changes water so that it becomes_____. ch: 2: verses 1-12.

Up:

14 - The_____is empty. ch: 20: verses 1-10.

18 - John the Baptist tells the_____about Jesus. ch: 1: verses 19-28.

21 - For God_____loved the world; ch: 3

29 - A Samaritan woman came to the_____. ch: 4: verses 1-26.

Up:(Backwards)

26 - Jesus explained why he washed their_____. ch: 13: verses 12-20.

27 - Jesus' trial in front of_____pilate. ch: 18: verses 28-37.

28 - John wanted his readers to believe that Jesus is the_____, God's son. (See reference page).

Acts

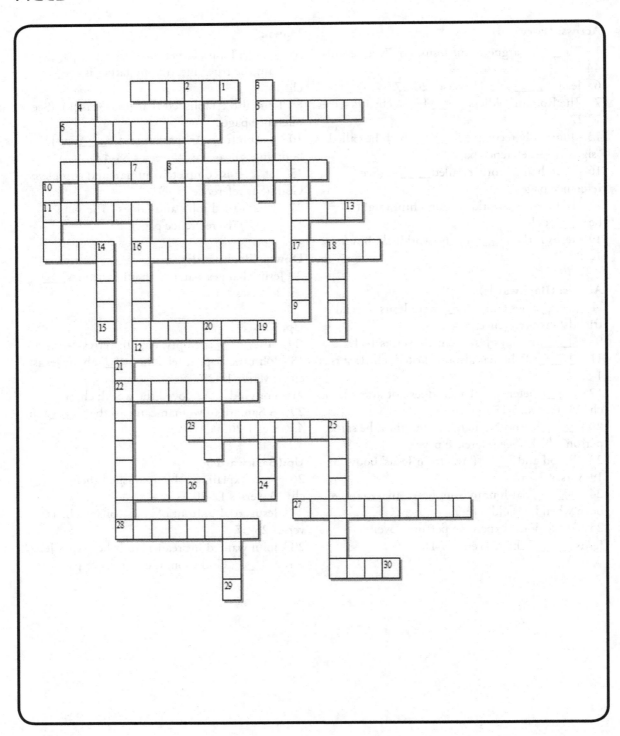

Acts - Questions

Across: (Forward)

5 - Stephen was full of the Holy Spirit, he turned his face towards_____. ch: 7: verses 54-60.

6 - Luke records that there about 120_____there. ch: 1: verses 15-20.

8 - When the day of_____was fully come. ch: 1: verses 1-4.

11 - _____; He used both words and actions to prophesy. ch: 21: verses 10-16.

16 - _____; Son of Sabbath. (See reference page).

17 - Paul and_____goes to Thessalonica. ch: 17: verses 1-4.

22 - _____; Festus wanted him to listen to Paul. ch: 25: verses 23-27.

23 - _____; A silversmith. ch: 19: verses 21-27.

27 - Acts tells the story of the first_____. (See reference page).

28 - Acts of the_____. (See reference page).

Across: (Backwards)

1 - Acts is the_____book in history that Luke wrote. ch: 1

7 - _____; Was the Governor of Judea. ch: 23: verses 26-30.

13 - _____; Persecutes the Christians. ch: 8: verses 1-4.

14 - _____; And Barnabas; But they shook off the dust of their feet against them. ch: 13: verses 42-52.

19 - _____; She was Felix's third wife. ch: 24: verses 24-27.

26 - _____; A man who does magic believes in Christ. ch: 8: verses 9-13.

30 - Ananias and Sapphira were husband and_____. ch: 5: verses 1-11.

Down:

2 - _____; A captain in the Roman army. ch: 10: verses 1-8.

3 - _____; Ekklesia. ch: 5: verses 12-16.

4 - _____; Howbeit they looked when he should have swollen. ch: 28: verses 1-10.

10 - The people try to kill_____. ch: 21: verses 27-36.

18 - _____; A seller of purple. ch: 16: verses 11-16.

20 - _____; was one of the 7 helpers. ch: 6: verses 8-15.

21 - Paul's vision about a man from_____. ch:16: verses 6-10

25 - Paul and Barnabas_____. They could not agree about John Mark. ch: 15: verses 36-41.

Up:

9 - The_____chose 7 men to help them. ch: 6: verses 1-7.

12 - And they called_____Jupiter. ch: 14: verses 8-13.

24 - A_____to kill Paul. ch: 23: verses 12-22.

29 - The author of Acts is_____. (See reference page).

Up: (Backwards)

15 - _____; Meets Cornelius. ch: 10:

Romans

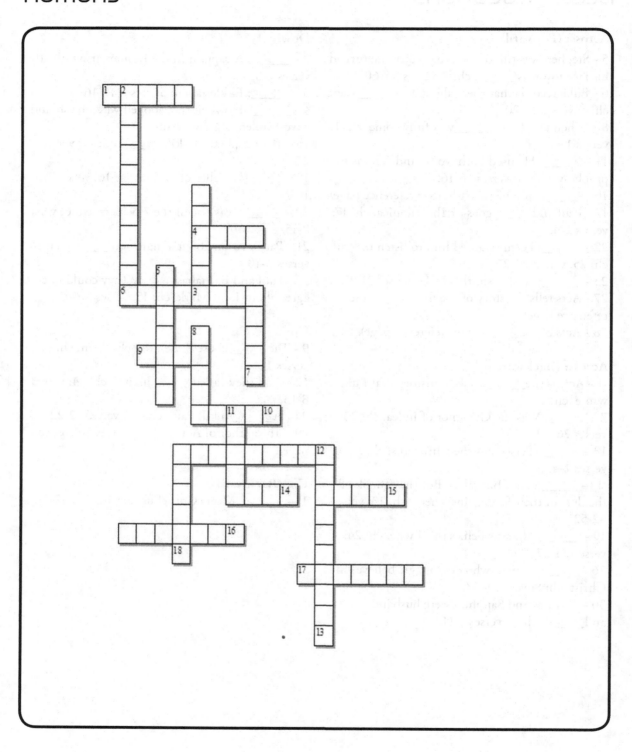

Romans - Questions

Across: (Forward)

1 - Two_____of slaves. ch: 6: verses 15-23.

4 - The book of Romans is a letter from_____to the Christians in Rome. (See reference page).

6 - The_____against sin. ch: 7: verses 14-25.

9 - The book of Romans shows us how God can save us from the punishment for our_____deeds. (See reference page).

17 - Every knee shall bow to me, and every tongue shall_____to God. ch: 14: verses 9-13.

Across: (Backwards)

10 - _____; A gift that nobody deserves. ch:1: verses 1-7.

12 - The_____that we receive because of God's grace. ch: 5: verses 1-11.

14 - _____; Had a vast army. (See reference page).

15 - And with the_____confession is made unto salvation. ch: 10: verses 8-11.

16 - The rulers of Rome were extremely powerful and_____. (See reference page).

Down:

2 - We then that are strong ought to bear the_____of the weak. ch: 15: verses 1-4.

5 - There were many Christians in Rome before Paul_____there. (See reference page).

8 - Paul described himself as a_____. ch: 1: verses 1-17.

11 - Dead to sin,_____in Christ. ch: 6: verses 1-14.

Up:

3 - Paul's words about the_____were bold and clear. ch: 1: verses 16-17.

7 - God will_____everyone, Jews and Gentiles. ch: 2: verses 12-16.

18 - Many_____had to work in Rome. (See reference page).

Up: (Backwards)

13 - A list of wicked_____. ch: 1: verses 28-32.

1st Corinthians

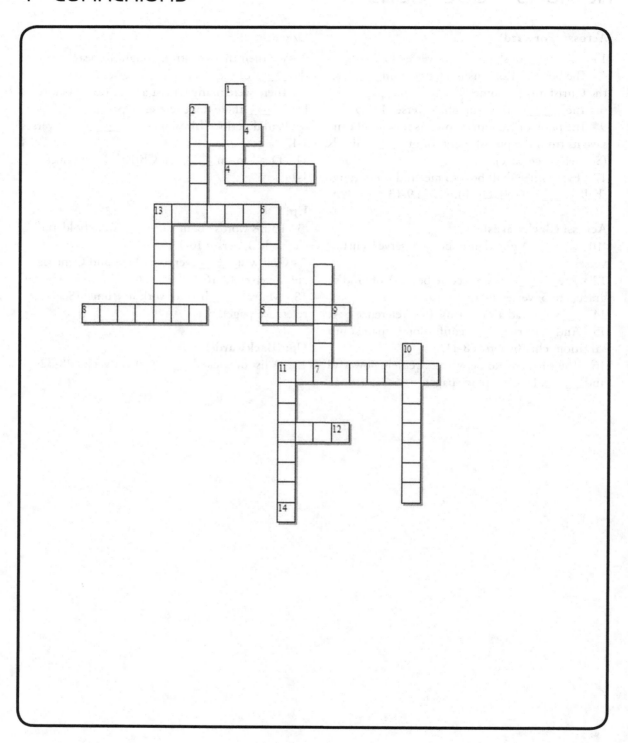

1st Corinthians - Questions

Across: (Forward)

8 - Paul calls the Christians his brothers and_____. ch: 2: verses 1-2.

11 - Is it not the_____of the blood of Christ? ch: 10: verses 16-17.

Across: (Backwards)

3 - Paul speaks about____groups. ch: 1: verse 12.

4 - The church and the_____. ch: 5: verses 9-13.

5 - _____; Was a city in the country of Greece. (See reference page).

9 - Paul also taught the people at Corinth that there is life after_____; (See reference page).

12 - _____; He wrote this first letter to the Christians who lived in the city of Corinth. (See reference page).

Down:

1 - The Christians at Corinth were very_____of their knowledge. ch: 3: verses 16-17.

2 - Take eat; This is my body which is_____for you. ch: 11: verses 24-26.

10 - Paul wanted to tell the people in Corinth how to praise God_____. (See reference page).

13 - The need to be_____. ch: 4: 6-13.

Up:

7 - For I would that all men were even as I_____. ch: 7: verses 6-9.

Up: (Backwards)

6 - But if there be no interpreter, let him keep silence in the_____. ch: 14:

14 - But when I became a man I put away_____ things. ch: 13:

2ⁿᵈCorinthians

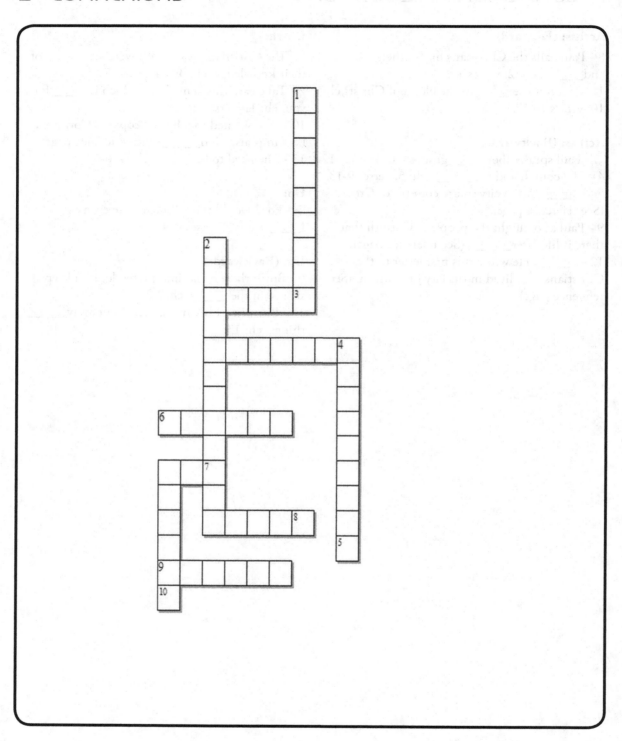

2ⁿᵈCorinthians - Questions

Across: (Forward)

6 - Paul wrote the_____called 2nd Corinthians. (See reference page).

9 - The city called Corinth was on a_____piece of land between northern and southern Greece. (See reference page).

Across: (Backwards)

3 - There was given to me a_____in the flesh; ch: 12: verse 7.

4 - _____; A person who God sent to teach the Christian message to the world. (See reference page).

7 - Some of the Christians at Corinth said_____ things about Paul. ch: 1:

8 - Paul explained that he had intended to visit them_____. ch: 1:

Down:

1 - For this is_____for you, who have begun before, not only to do, but also to be forward a year ago. chL 8: verse 10.

2 - But his bodily presence is weak, and his speech_____. ch: 10: verse 10.

Up:

10 - But though our outward man perish, yet the_____man is renewed day by day. ch: 4: verse 16.

Up: (Backwards)

5 - Paul talks about the old agreement and the new_____. ch: 3: verses 7-11.

Galatians

Galatians - Questions

Across: (Forward)

2 - _____; He wrote the book of Galatians. (See reference page).

8 - Galatia was part of the country thar we now call_____. (See reference page).

10 - And would_____the Gospel of Christ. ch: 1: verse 7.

12 - It was the_____for a person to write their name at the beginning of a letter. ch: 1:

Across: (Backwards)

3 - Paul showed_____that his behaviour was not reasonable. ch: 2: verses 13-14. (See reference page).

4 - _____; Someone who is not wise. ch: 3:

6 - Paul_____to agree with what the false teachers taught. ch: 2:

11 - Paul wrote in his letter how people should_____. (See reference page).

13 - Paul knew all about the Jewish_____. (See reference page).

Down:

1 - The book of_____is a letter. (See reference page).

5 - If we live in the_____, let us also walk in the spirit. ch: 5: verse 25.

7 - But he of the_____was by promise. ch: 4: verse 28.

14- For if a man think himself to be something, when he is nothing, he_____himself. ch: 6: verse 3.

Up:

9 - Paul wanted to emphasise to the Christians that he was a true_____. ch: 1:

Up: (Backwards)

15- _____; is every one that continueth not in all things which are written in the book of the law to do them. ch: 3: 10.

Ephesians

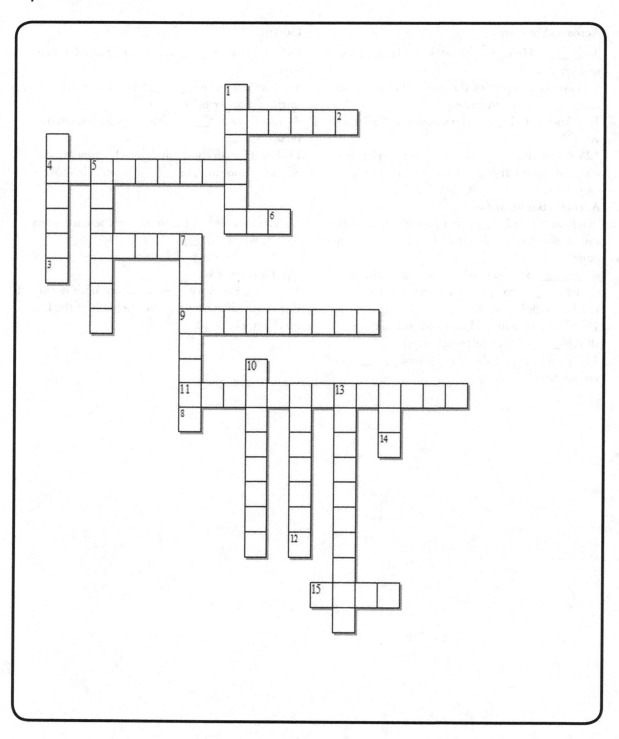

Ephesians - Questions

Across: (Forward)

4 - _____; Paul wrote this letter to the church at Ephesus. (See reference page).

9 - A_____way to live. ch: 4: verses 17-32.

11 - But_____what the will of the Lord is; ch: 5: verse 17.

15 - That we should be_____and without blame before him in love; ch: 1: verse 4.

Across: (Backwards)

2 - Put on the whole_____of God; ch: 6:

6 - The_____gave his life for us. ch: 1: verses 7-12.

7 - The_____of Christ. ch: 11: 7-12.

Down:

1 - When Paul wrote the book of Ephesians, Paul was in_____. (See reference page).

5 - He that loveth his wife loveth_____. ch: 5: verse 28.

10 - This letter is in two parts; 1. The place of the believer in Christ; 2. The behaviour of the_____ in the world. (See reference page).

13 - But bring them up in the nurture and_____ of the Lord. ch: 6:

Up:

3 - Jews and Gentiles are_____in Christ. ch: 2: verses 11-22.

8 - The one_____. ch: 2: verses 19-22.

12 - Children obey your_____in the Lord; ch: 6:

14 - This letter to the church at Ephesus was not a_____letter. (See reference page).

Philippians

Philippians - Questions

Across: (Forward)

2 - The plan to send_____. ch: 2: verses 19-24.

7 - I count not myself to have_____; ch: 3: verse 13.

9 - _____; Paul wrote this letter to the church at Philippi. (See reference page).

Across: (Backwards)

1 - Paul gives_____to God. ch: 1: verses 3-8.

3 - But my God shall supply all your_____ according to his riches in glory by Christ Jesus. ch: 4: verse 19.

8 - Timothy had been with Paul when he established the church at_____. ch: 1: verses 1-3.

Down:

5 - Paul urges the Christians at Philippi to fight together for the_____. ch: 1: verses 27-30.

Up:

4 - I_____toward the mark for the prize of the high calling of God in Christ Jesus; ch: 3: verse 14.

6 - Paul was a_____when he wrote the book of Philippians. (See reference page).

10 - The return of_____. ch: 2: verses 25-30.

Colossians

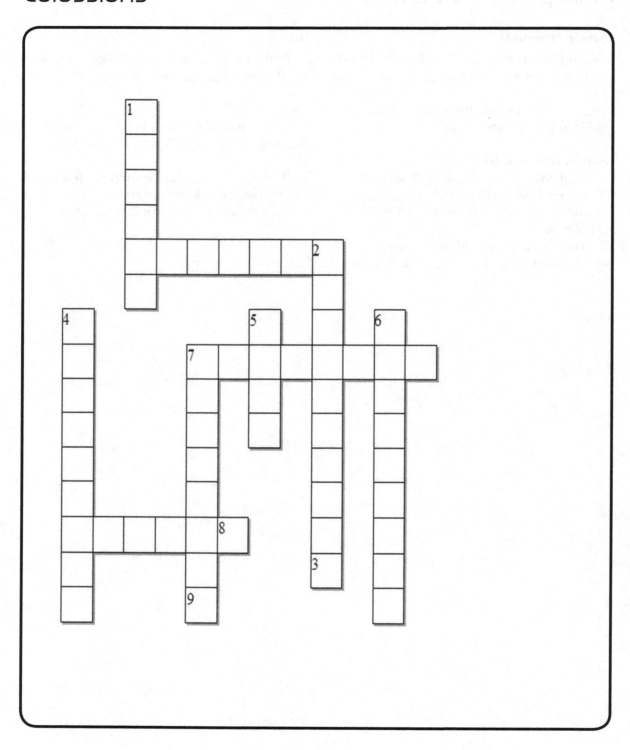

Colossians - Questions

Across: (Forward)

7 - Let your speech be alway with grace,_____ with salt. ch: 4: verse 6.

Across: (Backwards)

2 - _____; It was in the valley of the river Lycus. Today this part of the country is Turkey. (See reference page).

8 - Touch not, taste not,_____not. ch: 2: verses 20-23.

Down:

1 - Vainly_____up by his fleshly mind. ch: 2: verse 18.

4 - Anger, wrath, malice,_____, filthy communication out of your mouth. ch: 3: verses 6-10.

5 - That ye might_____worthy of the Lord unto all pleasing; ch: 1: verses 7-10.

6 - Always labouring_____for you in prayers, ch: 4: verse 12.

Up:

9- _____; was a minister, he visited Paul while Paul was in prison. (See reference page).

Up: (Backwards)

3 - Paul was in prison when he wrote the book of_____. (See reference page).

1st Thessalonians

1st Thessalonians – Questions

Across: (Forward)

1 - For the wrath is come upon them to the_____. ch: 2: verse 16.
3 - With the voice of the_____; ch: 4: verse 16.

Across: (Backwards)

5 - And how ye turned to God from_____to serve the living and true God. ch: 1: verse 9.
6 - When I could no longer_____, I sent to know your faith; ch: 3: verse 5.
8 - Paul,_____and Timothy were all in agreement with what the letter contained. (See reference page).

Down:

2 - _____; Paul wrote this letter to Christians in Thessalonica. (See reference page).

Down: (Backwards)

10 - But let us, who are of the day, be_____. ch: 5: verse 8.

Up:

4 - Because we would not be_____unto any of you; ch: 2: verse 9.
7 - We give thanks to God always for you_____, ch: 1: verse 2.

Up: (Backwards)

9 - _____from all appearance of evil. ch: 5: verse 22.

2nd Thessalonians

2ⁿᵈ Thessalonians - Questions

Across: (Forward)

2 - Wherefore we_____always for you. ch: 1: verse 11.

8 - Silas and Timothy are included in the_____. ch: 1: (See reference page).

Across: (Backwards)

4 - Let no man deceive you by any_____. ch: 2: verse 3.

6 - _____; He wrote this letter (2nd Thessalonians) to the Christians in Thessalonica. (See reference page).

7 - Yet count him not as an enemy but_____him as a brother. ch: 3: verse 15.

Down:

1 - Finally_____, pray for us; ch: 3: verse 1.

5 - In_____fire taking vengeance on them that know not God. ch: 1: verses 6-8.

Up:

3 - That they all might be_____who believed not the truth. ch: 2: verse 12.

1st Timothy

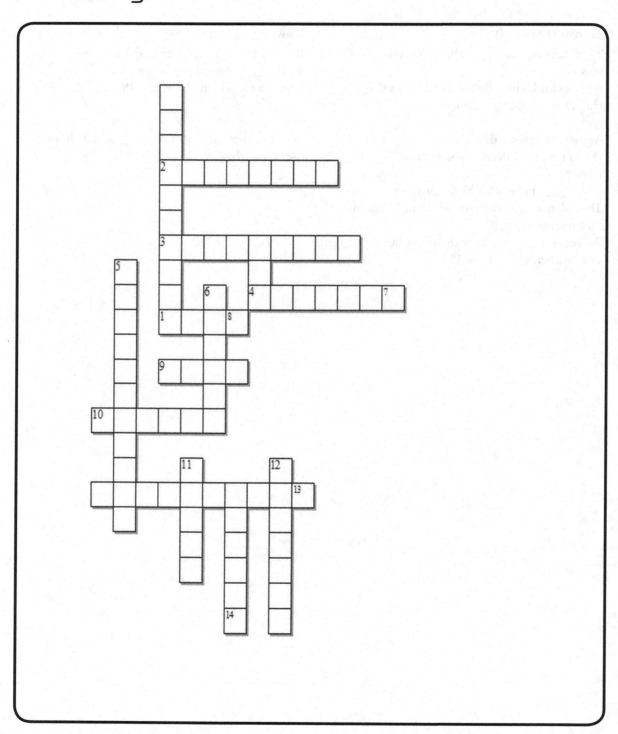

1st Timothy - Questions

Across: (Forward)

2 - In the letter Paul warned Timothy about false_____. (See reference page).

3 - Which some having put away concerning faith have made_____. ch: 1: verse 19.

9 - Timothy's Grandmother name was_____. (See reference page).

10 - Let the elders that rule well be counted worthy of_____honour. ch: 5: verse 17.

Across: (Backwards)

7 - That women adorn themselves in modest_____; ch: 2: verse 9.

8 - 1st Timothy is a letter that was written by_____. (See reference page).

13 - Charge them that are rich in this world, that they be not_____. ch: 6: verse 17.

Down:

5 - Neither give heed to fables and endless_____. ch: 1: verse 4.

6 - Timothy's mother name, was_____. (See reference page).

11 - And let these also_____be proved; ch: 3: verse 10.

12 - _____; was the son of a Gentile father and a Jewish mother. (See reference page).

Up:

1 - With the laying on of the hands of the_____. ch: 4: verse 14.

4 - The purpose of the_____. ch: 1: verses 8-11.

14 - How shall he take care of the_____of God? ch: 3: verse 5.

2nd Timothy

2nd Timothy – Questions

Across: (Forward)

2 - For_____in righteousness; ch: 3: verse 16.
4 - But especially the_____; ch: 4: verse 13.
10 - For if we be dead with him, we shall also_____with him. ch: 2: verse 11.
12 - Paul was in_____when he wrote his second letter to Timothy. (See reference page).

Across: (Backwards)

7 - I have kept the_____; ch: 4: verse 7.
9 - Paul knew that the time of his_____had come. (See reference page).
14 - Paul is lonely and the prison is_____. (See reference page).

Down:

5 - Paul ask Timothy to bring the warm_____ that he had left in the town of Troas. (See reference page).
6 - For men shall be lovers of their own_____. ch: 3: verse 2.
8 - Paul is_____to die. ch: 4: verses 6-8.
13 - Hold fast the form of_____words. ch: 1: verse 13.

Down: (Backwards)

1 - With them that call on the Lord out of a_____heart. ch: 2: verse 22.
11 - And is_____for doctrine. ch: 3: verse 16.

Up:

3 - All scripture is given by_____of God. ch: 3: verse 16.

Titus

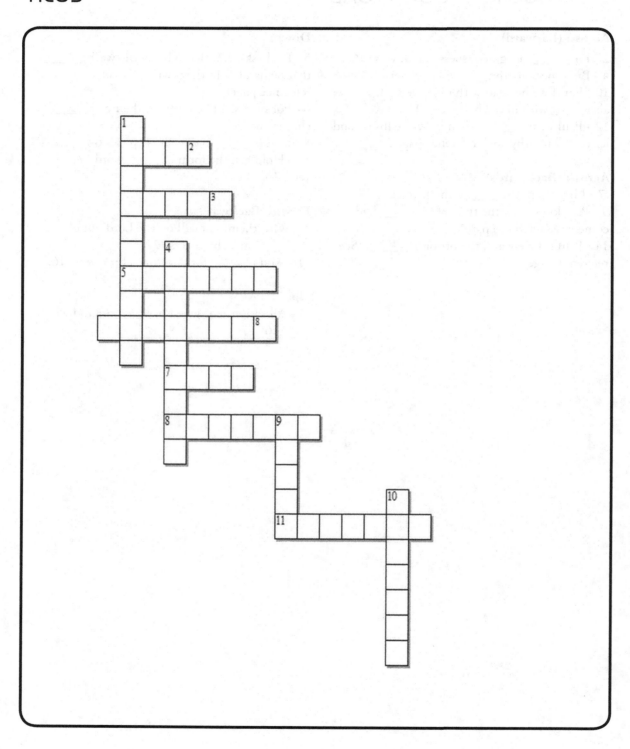

Titus – Questions

Across: (Forward)

5 - We should be made heirs according to the hope of_____life. ch: 3: verse 7.

6 - And purify unto himself a_____people. ch: 2: verse 14.

7 - Grace be with you all._____. ch: 3: verse 15.

11 - Titus had to organize the people in_____ who collected money for the poor people. (See reference page).

Across: (Backwards)

2 - _____; wrote the book of Titus. (See reference page).

3 - Paul advised_____how he should teach different groups of people; young, old and slaves. (See reference page).

8 - Title was a_____Christian. (See reference page).

Down:

1 - That the word of God be not_____. ch: 2: verse 5.

4 - Titus went to_____wity Paul. (See reference page).

10 - Whose mouths must be_____. ch: 1: verse 11.

Down: (Backwards)

9 - Titus was working on an Island called_____. ch: 1:

Philemon

Philemon - Questions

Across: (Forward)

1 - A brother_____. ch: 1: verse 16.

3 - _____him as myself. ch: 1: verse 17.

4 - _____; has run away from Philemon and has come to Paul. (See reference page).

5 - The book of Philemon is a short personal letter written by_____. (See reference page).

6 - Paul appealed to Philemon on behalf of Philemon's_____. (See reference page).

Down:

2 - My_____in Christ Jesus. ch: 1: verse 23.

Up:

7 - Refresh my_____in the Lord. ch: 1: verse 20.

Hebrews

Hebrews - Questions

Across: (Forward)

11 - Jesus is superior to_____. ch: 7: verses 1-28.

12 - Jesus is our_____. (See reference page).

13 - Jesus Christ the same_____and to day and for ever. ch: 13: verse 8.

Across: (Backwards)

2 - Whose voice then_____the earth, ch: 12: verse 26.

5 - Jesus is superior to_____in his person. ch: 1: verses 4-14.

6 - The book of Hebrews teaches that Jesus is God, but Jesus became a_____. ch: 1: (See reference page).

Down:

3 - The writer tries to show his readers that the right choice was to continue to trust in_____. (See reference page).

4 - Jesus is the_____priest. (See reference page).

7 - Let us lay_____every weight; ch: 12: verse 1.

8 - That he by the grace of God should_____ death for every man. ch: 2: verse 9.

Down:(Backwards)

1 - The_____of the book of Hebrews does not tell us his name. (See reference page).

Up:

9 - By faith the walls of_____fell down. ch: 11: verse 30.

10 - The_____of things not seen. ch: 11: verse 1.

James

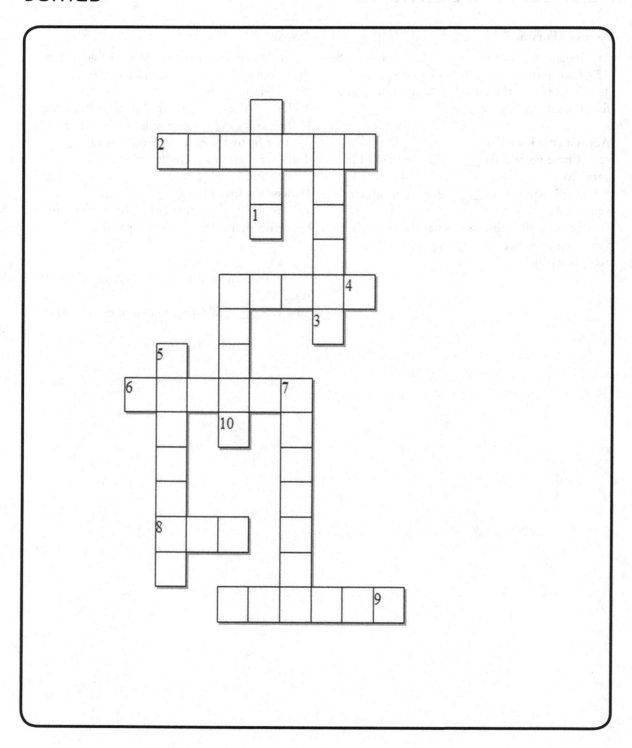

James – Questions

Across: (Forward)

2 - Let the brother of low degree rejoice in that he is_____. ch: 1: verse 9.

6 - It is even a_____, that appeareth for a little time. ch: 4: verse 14.

8 - But let your yea be yea and your_____be nay. ch: 5: verse 12.

Across: (Backwards)

4 - So faith without_____is dead also. ch: 2: verse 26.

9 - The book of James is a_____. (See reference page).

Down:

5 - Be_____therefore, brethren, unto the coming of the Lord. ch: 5: verse 7.

7 - But if ye have_____to persons, ye commit sin. ch: 2: verse 9.

Up:

1 - James was the_____brother of Jesus. (See reference page).

3 - And the_____is a fire, a world of iniquity. ch: 3: verse 6.

10- But be ye_____of the word and not hearer only. ch: 1: verse 22.

1st Peter

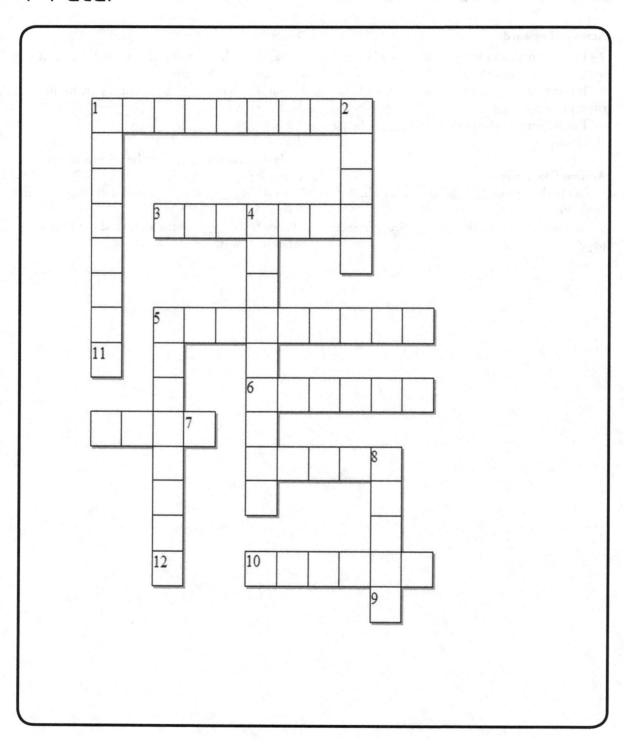

1st Peter – Questions

Across: (Forward)

1 - Peter wrote his letter to Christians who were_____. (See reference page).

3 - Or of putting on of_____; ch: 3: verse 3.

5 - Ye may be glad also, with_____joy. ch: 4: verse 13.

6 - Ye also, as lively_____. ch: 2: verse 5.

Across: (Backwards)

7 - Wherefore gird up the loins of your_____. ch: 1: verse 13.

8 - The author of 1st Peter was_____. (See reference page).

10 - 1st Peter is a_____. (See reference page).

Down:

2 - And his lips that they speak no_____; ch: 3: verse 10.

4 - Because your_____the Devil. ch: 5: verse 8.

Up:

12 - Peter was a_____of Jesus. (See reference page).

Up: (Backwards)

9 - _____; means a rock or stone. (See reference page).

11- _____; Helped Peter write this letter. ch: 5: verse 12. (See reference page).

2nd Peter

2nd Peter – Questions

Across: (Forward)

2 - _____; He wrote the 2nd Letter. (2nd Peter). (See reference page).

7 - Add to your faith_____; ch: 1: verse 5.

Across: (Backwards)

4 - Peter warned the Christians about evil_____. (See reference page).

6 - But_____in grace. ch: 3: verse 18.

Down: (Backwards)

1 - Peter was in the city of_____when he wrote the letter. (See reference page).

Up:

3 - And to reserve the unjust unto the day of_____to be punished. ch: 2: verse 9.

Up: (Backwards)

5 - Knowing that shortly I must put off this my_____. ch: 1: verse 14.

1st John

1st John - Questions

Across: (Forward)

3 - Because he first_____us. ch: 4: verse 19.

4 - For tWe_____, ch: 1: verse he_____was manifested; ch: 1: verse 2.

10 - Believe_____every spirit. ch: 4: verse 1.

12 - And the_____is not in him; ch: 2: verse 4.

13 - He that hath the_____hath life. ch: 5: verse 12.

Across: (Backwards)

8 - John wrote this letter to all_____. (See reference page).

9 - I_____unto you; ch: 2: verse 12.

11 - We_____, ch: 1: verse 6.

14 - When writing this letter, John was an_____ man. (See reference page).

Down:

1 - We make him a_____, ch: 1: verse 10.

2 - And_____one another. ch: 3: verse 23.

5 - John was the writer of the_____Gospel. (See reference page).

7 - For sin is the_____of the law. ch: 3: verse 4.

11 - John was in_____when he wrote this letter. (See reference page).

Up:

6 - John was one of the_____men to follow Jesus. (See reference page).

15 - And these_____agree in one. ch: 5: verse 8.

2nd John

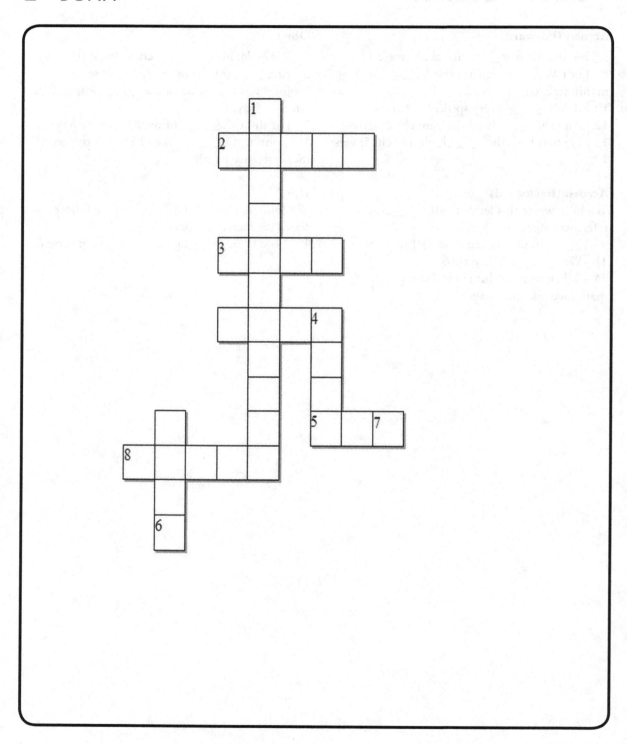

2nd John – Questions

Across: (Forward)

2 - Receive him not into your_____. ch: 1: verse 10.

3 - Ye should_____in it. ch: 1: verse 6.

8 - 2nd John was a_____letter. (See reference page).

Across: (Backwards)

4 - The elder unto the elect_____and, her children; ch: 1: verse 1.

7 - That our_____may be full. ch: 1: verse 12.

Down:

1 - This is the_____, ch: 1: verse 6.

Up:

6 - The author was_____who also wrote John's Gospel. (See reference page).

Up: (Backward)

5 - And now I beseech thee_____. ch: 1: verse 5.

3rd John

3ʳᵈ John - Questions

Across: (Forward)

5 - John called himself the_____. (See reference page).

Across: (Backwards)

3 - Follow not that which is_____. ch: 1: verse 11.

4 - _____; He did not agree with John. ch: 1: verses 8-9.

6 - _____be unto thee. ch: 1: verse 14.

7 - 3rd John is a personal letter from John to_____. (See reference page).

Down:

1 - That we might be_____to the truth. ch: 1: verse 8.

2 - John was_____to hear that Gaius was teaching God's message. (See reference page).

Jude

Jude - Questions

Across: (Forward)

1 - And speak evil of_____. ch: 1: verse 8.

3 - Jude was a brother of_____. (See reference page).

Across: (Backwards)

5 - _____men, ch: 1: verse 4.

10- For there are certain men_____in unawares, ch: 1: verse 4.

8 - Suffering the_____of eternal fire. ch: 1: verse 7.

9 - The_____of the book is Jude. (See reference page).

Down:

4 - To the only wise God our_____. ch: 1: verse 25.

6 - _____whose fruit withereth. ch: 1: verse 12.

7 - The book of Jude is a short_____in the Bible. (See reference page).

Up:

2 - Walking after their own_____. ch: 1: verse 16

Revelation

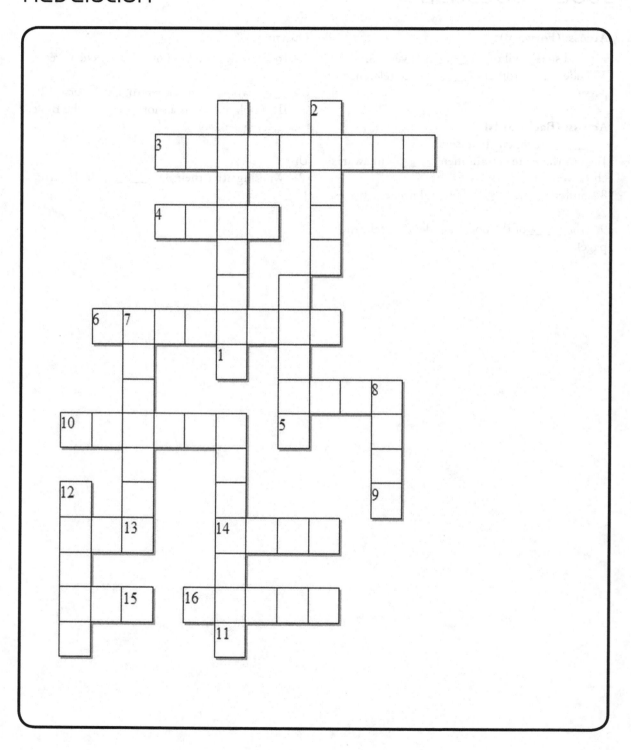

Revelation - Questions

Across: (Forward)

3 - Neither had received his mark upon their_____. ch: 20: verse 4.

4 - And the street of the_____was pure gold. ch: 21: verse 21.

6 - John calls this book a_____. (See reference page).

10 - The book of Revelation is a book about the_____. (See reference page).

14 - And every living_____died in the sea. ch: 16: verse 3.

16 - Jesus will win the fight against the_____. (See reference page).

Across: (Backwards)

8 - And I_____saw these things. ch: 22: verse 8.

13 - And he that sat on him had a_____. ch: 6: verse 2.

15 - Woe,_____,woe, ch: 8: verse 13.

Down:

2 - The purpose of this book is to show how_____will come again. (See reference page).

7 - Who also am your_____m ch: 1: verse 9.

12 - And it was in my mouth_____as honey. ch: 10: verse 10.

Up:

1 - And unto the angel of the church in_____; ch: 2: verse 18.

5 - I stand at the door and_____, ch: 3: verse 20.

9 - The author was_____who was a disciple of Jesus. (See reference page).

11 - A_____of wheat for a penny. ch: verse 6.

ANSWERS TO THE CROSSWORD PUZZLES

Genesis – Vol 3 Answers

Across (Forward)

3. Angel

4. Wealthy

7. Head

8. Leah

10. Fruitful

11. Preserve

14. Manasseh

15. Good

17. Moriah

19. Abimelech

22. Succoth

25. Name

26. Father

27. Naphtali

29. Food

30. Jacob

32. Age

33. First

Down (Downward)

1. Rebekah

2. Prostitutes

5. Raven

6. Slaves

9. Wife

12. Grain

16. Grace

18. Family

20. Light

21. Morning

23. Count

24. Benjamin

28. Abraham

31. Esau

Across (Backwards)

13. Bitumen

Up

34. Ark (Backwards)

35. Flood (Backwards)

36. Possessions (Backwards)

Exodus – Vol 3 Answers

Across (Forward)

8. Top
11. Jethro
21. Passover
23. Frogs
24. Meeting
28. Ahisamach
31. Eleazar

Down (Downward)

1. Tent
2. Mortar
3. Sticks
4. Ephod
13. Manna
14. First
26. Wall
29. Ice

Across (Backwards)

5. Hole
9. River
10. Stand
12. Gold
15. Face
16. Six
32. Special

Up

6. Death
7. Bones
17. Egypt
18. Stood
19. Glory
20. Numbers
22. Yard
25. Law
27. Lamps
30. Salt
33. Anyone
34. Second

Leviticus – Vol 3 Answers

Across (Forward)

6. Hyssop

8. Sin

10. Bless

12. Goel

14. Respect

18. Molech

Down (Downward)

1. Devote

3. Holy

5. Seven (Backwards)

7. Offering

15. Priests

19. Law

22. Buggery (Backwards)

Across (Backwards)

4. Atonement

11. Fire

17. Blasphemy

20. Beat

Up

9. Corn

13. Peace

16. Clean

21. Bled (Backwards)

Numbers – Vol 3 Answers

Across (Forward)

4. Behalf
8. Second
10. Twelve
20. Water
24. Guard
25. Peor
27. Passover
28. Miriam

Down (Downward)

1. Zelophehad
5. Wrote
9. Sacrifices
15. Married
16. Families
19. Spoils
21. Fairly
22. Tassels
32. Shelters

Across (Backwards)

3. Harvest
7. Wearing
11. Safe
13. All
14. Desert
17. Female
18. Lists
23. Israelites
26. Chapter

Up

2. Promise
6. Body
12. Prophesied
29. Egypt
30. Sheol (Backwards)
31. Promise

Deuteronomy – Vol 3 Answers

Across (Forward)

1. Cow
11. Life
12. Jordan
15. Man
23. Weeks

20. Mouth (backwards)
22. Sons
24. Stones (backwards)
27. Tents

Down (Downward)

2. Obey
3. Moses
4. Obey (Backwards)
10. Climbed
14. Prophets
17. King

Across (Backwards)

5. Deuteronomy
9. Debt
16. Rules
18. Three
21. Good
25. Satan
26. Last
28. Words

Up

7. False
8. Love
13. Food
19. Report

Joshua – Vol 3 Answers

Across (Forward)

4. Gibeon

5. Swords

7. Refuge

9. Herron

10. Prayer

11. Achan

13. Geliloth

16. Reads

21. Zebulun

Down (Downward)

2. Lord

3. Amorites

6. Caleb (Backwards)

8. Ephraim

12. Joseph (Backwards)

14. Promise (Backwards)

15. Small (Backwards)

17. Reminded (Backwards)

18. Faith

19. Canaan

Across (Backwards)

1. Moses

20. Alamekites

22. River

Up

23. Instructions

Judges – Vol 3 Answers

Across (Forward)

5. Seemed
7. Beliefs
9. Disappear
11. Turn
15. King
16. Wise
17. Complained

Down (Downward)

1. Jobs
3. Jael
8. Concubine (Backwards)
10. Syria (Backwards)
14. Twelve

Across (Backwards)

4. Baals
6. Bethal
12. Shamgar
18. Villages
19. Jawbone

Up

1. Millstone
13. Success (Backwards)
20. Bridge (Backwards)

Ruth - Vol 3 Answers

Across (Forward)

12. Perez

3. Barley (Backwards)

8. Redeem (Backwards)

10. Ruth

Down (Downward)

2. Naomi (Backwards)

Across (Backwards)

1. Six

4. Obed

5. Woman

7. Lay

9. Elders

11. Grain

UP

6. Widow

13. Glean

1st Samuel – Vol 3 Answers

Across (Forward)

3. Refuses

12. Samuel

14. Gives

15. Jealous

10. Write

11. David

Down (Downward)

2. Dies

4. Sons

7. Goliath (backwards

9. Donkeys

Across (Backwards)

5. Left

8. Ark

13. First

16. Judges

UP

1. Centuries

6. Kill

2nd Samuel – Vol 3 Answers

Across (Forward)

6. Amalekite

8. Shields

15. Absalom

Down (Downward)

1. Bathsheba

3. Defeated

5. Jerusalem

7. Nobody (Backwards)

11. Rabbah (Backwards)

Across (Backwards)

10. Mephibosheth

14. King

Up

2. Israelites

4. Praises

9. Sister

12. Wars

13. Book

16. Alter (Backwards)

1st Kings – Vol 3 Answers

Across (Forward)

1. Jeroboam

3. Dangerous

4. Wives

5. Wisdom

14. Asherah

17. After

Down (Downward)

2. Adonijah

6. Solomon

10. Two (Backwards)

13. Israel (backwards)

15. Sorry

16. Judah (Backwards)

Across (Backwards)

7. History

9. Rehoboam

12. Tent

Up

8. Box (Backwards)

11. Palace

18. Feed

2nd Kings – Vol 3 Answers

Across (Forward)

3. Nebuzaradan

5. Jehu

6. Sins

9. Heaven

10. Naaman

Down (Downward)

1. Hezekiah

2. Baal

4. Elisha (Backwards)

15. Axe

Across (Backwards)

8. Fire

11. Judah

14. Athaliah

Up

7. Refused (Backwards)

12. Child

13. Safe

16. Joash

1st Chronicles – Vol 3 Answers

Across (Forward)

1. Ram

3 .Experts

5. Thanks

7. Family

9. Hiram

10. Israelites

13. Shaharaim

Down (Downward)

2.Aaron

6.Meunites (Backwards)

8. Chronicles

11. Jehoiachi

14. Moses

Across (Backwards)

15. Levite

Up

4. Names

12. History

16. Ezra

17. Last

2ⁿᵈ Chronicles – Vol 3 Answers

Across (Forward)

3. Solomon

4. Rehoboam

9. Septuagint

11. Separates

14. Sennacherib

16. Sheba

17. Temple

Down (Downward)

1. Tarshish

5. Book

7. Jehoshaphat

8. Rule

10. Fills

15. Exile (Backwards)

Across (Backwards)

2. Translation

6. Proud

Up

12. Asa

13. Years

Ezra – Vol 3 Answers

Across (Forward)

3. Jerusalem

7. Teach

Down (Downward)

2. Seventh

5. Shecaniah (Backwards)

6. Persia

8. Judah

9. Foreign

Across (Backwards)

10. Darius

11. Artaxerxes

12. Babylonia

Up

1. Cyrus

4. Three

Nehemiah – Vol 3 Answers

Across (Forward)
2. Defence
13. Shemaiah
14. Eliashib

Down (Downward)
6. Same
9. Nehemiah
10. Skilled
16. Nethinims

Across (Backwards)
3. Hanani
4. Noadiah
8. Trade
11. Tobiah

Up
1. Sincere
5. Ezra
7. City
12. Chief
15. Married

Esther – Vol 3 Answers

Across (Forward)

4. Believed
5. Property
8. Plotted

Down (Downward)

1. Hammedatha
3. Jewish
9. Esther
10. Shaashgaz

Across (Backwards)

7. Mordecai
11. Name
12. Susa
13. Square

Up

2. Officials
6. Obey
14. Xerxes
15. Sleep

Job – Vol 3 Answers

Across (Forward)

7. Nations

8. Tree

12. Voice

14. Discuss

19. Elihu

Down (Downward)

4. Wisdom

5. Angry

6. Job

20. Dream

Across (Backwards)

2. Wife

3. List

10. Animals

11. Bildad

16. Suffering

17. End

21. Accuser

Up

1. Trusted

9. Zophar

13. Before

15. Hedge

18. Lawyer

22. Troubles

Psalm – Vol 3 Answers Part One

Across (Forward)

2. Rescue

5. Higgaion

7. Collection

14. Morning

16. Sweeter

Down (Downward)

1. Cush

4. David

9. Ill

10. Nabal

11. Sad

13. Protect

15. Israel

Across (Backwards)

6. Praise

12. Repeats

17. Secret

Up

3. Overflows

8. Sceptre

18. Answer

Psalm - Vol 3 Answers Part Two

Across (Forward)

3. Korah

8. Wings

Down (Downward)

2. Free (Backwards)

4. Help

6. Stress (Backwards)

Across (Backwards)

1. Selah

5. Maskil

9. Disgrace

11. Hate

Up

7. Mediterranean (Backwards)

10. Hiding

Psalm – Vol 3 Answers Part Three

Across (Forward)

5. Bathsheba

6. Sheol

9. Ziph

12. Sennacherib

13. Hear

Down (Downward)

1. Judge

3. Snake (Backwards)

7. Earthquake (Backwards)

11. Penitential

Across (Backwards)

2. Depressed

8. Uriah

Up

4. Deep

10. Betray

Psalm – Vol 3 Answers Part Four

Across (Forward)

2. Gracious

6. Royal

9. Bad

20. Elohim

Down (Downward)

3. Godless (Backwards)

5. Jacob

8. Adonai

11. Temple

Across (Backwards)

4. Covenant

7. Feast

Up

1. Fury

Psalm – Vol 3 Answers Part Five

Across (Forward)

2. Judge

6. Righteous

10. Praise

12. Tribes

13. Pitieth

Down (Downward)

3. Wineskin

5. Froward

7. Tongue (Backwards)

8. Oppressors

11. Tempted

Across (Backwards)

4. Zion

14. Grapes

15. Thrones

Up

1. Hallelujah

9. Wicked

Psalm – Vol 3 Answers Part Six

Across (Forward)

2. Hail

6. Snare

11. Trap

13. Dew

Down (Downward)

1. Slanderer

3. Awe

5. Viper

10. Angel

Across (Backwards)

8. Proud

9. Calm

14. Oil

15. Path

16. Lips

Up

4. Mount

7. Book

12. Harp

17. Dreaming (Backwards)

Proverbs – Vol 3 Answers

Across (Forward)

4. Wisdom

8. Acur

9. Difference

14. Dark

16. Trouble

Down (Downward)

1. Two

3. Skilled

7. Bribes

10. Four

11. Nothing

15. Woman

17. Lion

Across (Backwards)

2. Foolish

12. Our

13. Crops

Up

5. Bed

6. Farm

18. Married

19. Mistakes

Ecclesiastes – Vol 3 Answers

Across (Forward)

7. Age

8. Son

11. Teacher

Down (Downward)

1. Ecclesiastes

4. Honest

6. Wise (Backwards)

12. Right

Across (Backwards)

2. Die

5. People

10. Writer

Up

3. End

9. Happen

Song of Solomon – Vol 3 Answers

Across (Forward)

1.Shulamite

6. Word

8. Mandrake

9. Right

11. Virgin

Down (Downward)

4. Mare (Backwards)

5. Love

7. Waist

Across (Backwards)

2. Lebanon

13. Poem

14. Party

Up

3. Woman

10. Meeting

12. Description

15. Songs (Backwards)

Isaiah – Vol 3 Answers

Across (Forward)

3. Rahab

6. Amos

8. Pictures

14. Palace

17. Vineyard

19. Saves

Down (Downward)

1. Thoughts

2. Abraham (Backwards)

5. Northern

7. Arm

11. Omri

13. Frankincense

Across (Backwards)

4. Uzziah

9. Sword

16. Rise

18. Pain

Up

10. Idols

12. Renew

20. Politics (Backwards)

21. Prophet (Backwards)

Jeremiah- Vol 3 Answers

Across (Forward)

3. Mouth

7. Faces

8. Fire

13. Cells

15. Urijah

Down (Downward)

4. Jeremiah

5. Partridge

10. Child

12. Obominations

Across (Backwards)

6. Manasseh

9. Baruch

11. Baalim

Up

1.Wormwood

2.Firstfruits

14. Stumblingblocks

Lamentations – Vol 3 Answers

Across (Forward)

5. Writer

7. Stopped

9. Foxes

Down (Downward)

1. Zedekiah

4. Jeremiah

Across (Backwards)

2. Places

3. Jerusalem

6. Horn

Up

8. Food

10. Sad (Backwards)

11. Woman

Ezekiel – Vol 3 Answers

Across (Forward)

7. Posts

9. Paramours

12. Wind

13. Divination

16. Sin

17. Scroll

19. Coals

20. New

22. Future

23. Inside

Down (Downward)

1. Ezekiel

2. Jerusalem

4. Hophra

9. Oblation

14. Idumaea

15. Oholah

18. Look

Across (Backwards)

3. Cheurebim

6. Light

8. Zadok

21. Sea

25. Throne

Up

5. False

11. Cuts

24. Buzz

26. Strength (Backwards)

28. Person (Backwards)

Daniel – Vol 3 Answers

Across (Forward)

3. White

5. Antioch

6. Image

7. Times

17. Kingdoms

18. Tree

Down (Downward)

1. Education

2. Chose

4. Three (Backwards)

8. Second

11. First

15. Long

16. God

Across (Backwards)

10. Goat

12. Red

14. Four

Up

9. Fourth

13. Belshazzar

Hosea – Vol 3 Answers

Across (Forward)

3. Marry

8. Judge

12. Tabor

15. Roar

Down (Downward)

6. Israel

13. Covenant

18. Similitudes

Across (Backwards)

1. Baker

5. Prostitute

9. Idols

10. Hosea

14. Stone

Up

2. Blessings (Backwards)

4. Gomer

7. Priests (Backwards)

11. Hesed (Backwards)

16. Jeroboam

17. Jezreel (Backwards)

Joel – Vol 3 Answers

Across (Forward)

4. Years

5. Locusts

6. Grape

7. Eden

12. Mountains

14. Joel

15. Enemies

Down (Downward)

1. Drunks

9. Powerful

11. Wiser

Across (Backwards)

2. Dry

8. Repent

10. Noise

Up

3. Together

13. Jehoshaphat

16. Lord (Backwards)

Amos – Vol 3 Answers

Across (Forward)

2. Prophet

11. Damascus

Down (Downward)

1. Behaviors

3. Heavy

5. True

7. Tekoa

9. Amasiah

10. Gaza

Across (Backwards)

6. Exile

8. Sheep

12. Cause

Up

4. Weight

13. People (Backwards)

Obadiah - Vol 3 Answers

Across (Forward)

7. Judgement

Down (Downward)

1. Greater
3. Destruction
4. Shortest

Across (Backwards)

2. Obadiah
6. Loyal
8. Evil

Up

5. Family
9. Edom (Backwards)

Jonah – Vol 3 Answers

Across (Forward)

1. Swallow

6. Right

10. Sailors

14. Mouth

Down (Downward)

3. Lots

5. Prophet

7. Sleeping (Backwards)

9. Disobeyed

11. Sackcloth

13. Jonah

Across (Backwards)

4. Storm

8. Enemy

12. Joppa

16. Nineveh

Up

2. Threw

15. Ship

Micah – Vol 3 Answers

Across (Forward)

3. Travail

7. Minor

11. Morasthite

Down (Downward)

1. Village

2. Yahweh

4. Minor (Backwards)

9. Soothsayers

10. Brier

Across (Backwards)

5. Message

Up

6. Weeps

8. Suffer

12. Judgement

Nahum – Vol 3 Answers

Across (Forward)

1. Nineveh
6. Fortified
9. Rivers

Down (Downward)

2. Vengeance
3. Huzzab
8. Emptiers

Across (Backwards)

5. Imagine
11. Jealous

Up

4. Woman
7. Bruit
10. Whoredoms

Habakkuk – Vol 3 Answers

Across (Forward)

4. Own

6. Measured

10. Chaldeans

14. Animals

Down (Downward)

2. Prophet

5. Cruel (Backwards)

7. Suffer

8. Babylonians

12. Twice

13. Habakkuk

Across (Backwards)

1. Egypt

15. Recue

Up

3. Wine

9. Bad

11. Red

Zephaniah – Vol 3 Answers

Across (Forward)

1. Flocks

4. Masters

5. God

9. Zephaniah

11. Wait

Down (Downward)

2. Carelessly

3. Glad (Backwards)

6. Cherethites

Across (Backwards)

10. Filthy

13. Punish

Up

7. Hand

8. Baal

12. Undo

Haggai – Vol 3 Answers

Across (Forward)

2. Chariots

4. Drought

5. Signet

7. Shake

Down (Downward)

1. Glory

Across (Backwards)

8. Eyes

9. Barn

Up

3. Holes

6. Prophet

10. Rebuild

Zechariah – Vol 3 Answers

Across (Forward)

3. Prophet

5. Horse

7. Diviners

13. Hadadrimmon

18. Bastard

Down (Downward)

1. Zechariah

2. Lampstand

8. Speech

16. Basket (Backwards)

Across (Backwards)

4. Future

9. Prophecy

11. Jerusalem

14. Four

15. Gates

17. Vision

20. Scroll

Up

6. Remembers

10. Chief

12. Horses

19. Horns (Backwards)

Malachi – Vol 3 Answers

Across (Forward)
4. Malachi
8. Doors

Across (Backwards)
6. Esau
10. Messenger

Down (Downward)
2. Jacob
3. Tithes
5. Calves
9. Levi

Up
1. Jacob
7. Edom
11. Sin

Matthew – Vol 3 Answers

Across (Forward)

2. Love

3. Jesus

5. Feeds

13. Sadducees

16. Mount

11. Prayer

23. Mark

26. Son

27. Gospel

28. Pharisee

29. Caesar

Down (Downward)

1. Power

7. Christ

10. Mary (Backwards)

11. Baptism (Backwards)

15. People (Backwards)

17. Disciples

18. Special

19. Sanhedrin

24. Taught

30. Abraham

Across (Backwards)

12. First

8. Bethlehem

21. Baptist

25. Taxes

31. Mark

Up

4. Righteousness

6. Tests

9. Birth (Backwards)

14. Bread

20. Ten

32. Testament

33. Supper (Backwards)

Mark - Vol 3 Answers

Across (Forward)

1. ABBA
8. Daughter
11. Human
12. Life
14. Galilee
18. Plot
20. Choose
25. Antipas
26. Andrew

Down (Downward)

2. Beelzebub
7. Immediately
9. Apostle
10. Gospel
13. Walks
15. Mark
16. Zebedee
21. Aramatic (Backwards)

Across (Backwards)

3. Messenger
5. Son
17. Barnabas
22. Physically
24. Rock
27. Wife

Up

4. Denies
6. Stone
19. Divorce
23. Boy

Luke – Vol 3 Answers

Across (Forward)

2. Whole

6. Disciples

9. Lazarus

12. Mustard

17. Brokenhearted

19. Pilate

23. Antioch

24. Jesus

Down (Downward)

1. Forgive

4. Offering

5. Baptizes

7. Companion

16. Carried

18. Arimathea

20. Ghost

Across (Backwards)

3. Jesus

11. Midnight

14. Luke

15. Unclean

21. Sowed

Up

8. Gentle

10. Zacchaeus

13. Acts

22. Two

26. Old

27. Mary (Backwards)

John – Vol 3 Answers

Across (Forward)

1. People
6. Weeds
7. Crucify
13. Miracles
16. James
17. Saved
19. Light

Down (Downward)

2. Wine (Backwards)
3. Zebedee
5. Husbandman
8. Human
10. Nicodemus
15. Jesus
22. Thunder

Across (Backwards)

4. John
9. Judas
11. Word
12. Simon
20. Bartholomew
23. Water
24. Nicodemus
25. Feet

Up

14. Grave
18. People
21. So
26. Feet (Backwards)
27. Pontius (Backwards)
28. Messiah (Backwards)
29. Well

Acts – Vol 3 Answers

Across (Forward)

5. Heaven

6. Believers

8. Pentecost

11. Agabus

16. Barsabas

17. Silas

22. Aggrippa

23. Demetrius

27. Christians

28. Apostles

Down (Downward)

2. Cornelius

3. Church

4. Melita

10. Paul

18. Lydia

20. Stephen

21. Macedonia

25. Separate

Across (Backwards)

1. Second

7. Felix

13. Saul

14. Paul

19. Drusilla

26. Simon

30. Wife

Up

9. Apostles

12. Barnabas

15. Peter (Backwards)

24. Plot

29. Luke

Romans – Vol 3 Answers

Across (Forward)

1. Kinds
4. Paul
6. Struggle
9. Evil
17. Confess

Down (Downward)

2. Infirmities
5. Arrived
8. Slave
11. Alive

Across (Backwards)

10. Grace
12. Blessings
14. Rome
15. Mouth
16. Wealthy

Up

3. Gospel
7. Judge
13. Behaviours (Backwords)
18. Slaves

1st Corinthians – Vol 3 Answers

Across (Forward)

8. Sisters

11. Communion

Down (Downward)

1. Proud

2. Broken

10. Together

13. Humble

Across (Backwards)

3. Four

5. Corinth

9. Death

12. Paul

Up

6. Church (Backwards)

7. Myself

14. Childish Backwards)

2nd Corinthians – Vol 3 Answers

Across (Forward)

6. Letter

9. Narrow

Down (Downward)

1. Expedient

Across (Backwards)

3. Thorn

4. Apostle

7. Bad

8. Twice

Up

5. Agreement (Backwards)

10. Inward

Galatians – Vol 3 Answers

Across (Forward)

2. Paul

8. Turkey

10. Pervert

12. Custom

Down (Downward)

1. Galatians

5. Spirit

7. Freewoman

14. Deceiveth

Across (Backwards)

3. Peter

4. Foolish

6. Refused

11. Live

13. Laws

Up

9. Apostle

15. Cursed (Backwards)

Ephesians - Vol 3 Answers

Across (Forward)

4. Ephesians

9. Different

11. Understanding

15. Holy

Down (Downward)

1. Prison

5. Himself

10. Believer

13. Admonition

Across (Backwards)

2. Armour

6. Son

7. Gifts

Up

3. United

8. Building

12. Parents

14. Sad

Philippians – Vol 3 Answers

Across (Forward)

2. Timothy

7. Apprehended

9. Philippians

15. Holy

Down (Downward)

5. Faith

Across (Backwards)

1. Thanks

3. Need

8. Philippi

Up

4. Press

6. Prisoner

10. Epaphroditus

Colossians – Vol 3 Answers

Across (Forward)

7. Seasoned

Down (Downward)

1. Puffed

4. Blasphemy

5. Walk

6. Fervently

Across (Backwards)

2. Colosse

8. Handle

Up

3. Colossians (Backwards)

9. Epaphras

1st Thessalonians – Vol 3 Answers

Across (Forward)

1. Uttermost

3. Archangel

Down (Downward)

2. Thessalonians

10. Sober

Across (Backwards)

5. Idols

6. Forbear

8. Silas

Up

4. Chargeable

7. All

9. Abstain (Backwards)

2nd Thessalonians – Vol 3 Answers

Across (Forward)

2. Pray

8. Greeting

Down (Downward)

1. Brethren

5. Flaming

Across (Backwards)

4. Means

6. Paul

7. Admonish

Up

3. Damned

1st Timothy – Vol 3 Answers

Across (Forward)

2. Teachers

3. Shipwreck

9. Lois

10. Double

Down (Downward)

5. Genealogies

6. Eunice

11. First

12. Timothy

Across (Backwards)

7. Apparel

8. Paul

13. Highminded

Up

1. Presbytery

4. Law

14. Church

2nd Timothy – Vol 3 Answers

Across (Forward)

2. Instruction
4. Parchments
10. Live
12. Prison

Down (Downward)

1. Pure (Backwards)
5. Coat
6. Selves
8. Ready
11. Profitable (Backwards)
13. Sound

Across (Backwards)

7. Faith
9. Death
14. Cold

Up

3. Inspiration

Titus – Vol 3 Answers

Across (Forward)

5. Eternal

6. Peculiar

7. Amen

11. Corinth

Down (Downward)

1. Blasphemed

4. Jerusalem

9. Crete (Backwards)

10. Stopped

Across (Backwards)

2. Paul

3. Titus

8. Gentile

Philemon – Vol 3 Answers

Across (Forward)

1. Beloved

3. Receive

4. Onesimus

5. Paul

6. Slave

Down (Downward)

2. Fellow Prisoner

Up

7. Bowels (Backwards)

Hebrews – Vol 3 Answers

Across (Forward)

11. Melchisedec

12. Priest

13. Yesterday

Down (Downward)

1. Author (Backwards)

3. Jesus

4. Perfect

7. Aside

8. Taste

Across (Backwards)

2. Shook

5. Angels

6. Man

Up

9. Jericho

10. Evidence

James – Vol 3 Answers

Across (Forward)

2. Exalted

6. Vapour

8. Nay

Down (Downward)

5. Patient

7. Respect

Across (Backwards)

4. Works

9. Letter

Up

1. Half

3. Tongue

1st Peter – Vol 3 Answers

Across (Forward)

1. Suffering

3. Apparel

5. Exceeding

6. Stones

Down (Downward)

2. Guile

4. Adversary

Across (Backwards)

7. Mind

8. Peter

10. Letter

Up

9. Peter (Backwards)

11. Silvanus (Backwards)

12. Disciple

2nd Peter – Vol 3 Answers

Across (Forward)

2. Peter

7. Virtue

Down (Downward)

1. Rome (Backwards)

Across (Backwards)

4. Teachers

6. Grow

Up

3. Judgement

5. Tabernacle (Backwards)

1st John – Vol 3 Answers

Across (Forward)

3. Loved

4. Life

10. Not

12. Truth

13. Son

Down (Downward)

1. Liar (Backwards)

2. Love (Backwards)

5. Fourth

7. Transgression

Across (Backwards)

8. Christians

9. Write

11. Lie

14. Old

Up

6. First

15. Three

2nd John – Vol 3 Answers

Across (Forward)

2. House

3. Walk

8. Short

Down (Downward)

1. Commandment

Across (Backwards)

4. Lady

7. Joy

Up

5. Lady (Backwards)

6. John

3rd John – Vol 3 Answers

Across (Forward)

5. Elder

Down (Downward)

1. Fellowhelpers

2. Glad

Across (Backwards)

3. Evil

4. Diotrephes

6. Peace

7. Gaius

Jude – Vol 3 Answers

Across (Forward)

1. Dignities

3. Jesus

Down (Downward)

4. Saviour

6. Trees

7. Letter

Across (Backwards)

5. Ungodly

8. Vengeance

9. Author

10. Crept

Up

2. Lusts

Revelation – Vol 3 Answers

Across (Forward)

3. Foreheads
4. City
6. Prophecy
10. Future
14. Soul
16. Devil

Down (Downward)

2. Jesus
7. Brother (Backwards)
12. Sweet

Across (Backwards)

8. John
13. Bow
15. Woe

Up

1. Thyatira
5. Knock
9. John (backwards)
11. Measure

References

Bryant, T. Alton, Zondervan's Compact Bible Dictionary, June 1, 2001

Baker Publishing Group, New Combined Bible Dictionary and Concordance (Direction Bks), June 1, 1973

Godwin, Johnnie, Phyllis Godwin & Karen Dockery, The Student Bible Dictionary Jan 1, 2001

Merriam-Webster Dictionary, copyright 2011.

Spence, H.D.M & Joseph S. Exell. The Pulpit Commentary, 1985.

DR VBS MINISTRIES

"Growth Is A Necessity For Life"

Web site: www.drvbsministries.com

E-mail: vbs@drvbsministries.com

Unwittingly Hope

In his third volume, Dr. Verdree B. Stanley says life situations are not always manifested from left to right and from bottom upwards. Circumstances sometimes require a person to start at the end and work their way to the beginning or start from the top and work their way down to the bottom. Sometimes acquiring a goal is determine by the point of reference. A straight line is not always the shortest distance and a circle does not always connect. Each of the seventy-one crossword puzzles has its own unique design and will enhance growth in an individual's life.

DR VBS MINISTRIES
"Growth Is A Necessity For Life"
Web site: www.drvbsministries.com
E-mail: vbs@drvbsministries.com